Robert W. Finkel, Ph.D. (New York University), is a theoretical physicist and Chairman of the Department of Physics at St. John's University in New York. He is a consultant to industry and government and has published articles on physics, mathematics, biology, and education. Dr. Finkel also teaches workshops in practical techniques for learning and remembering at the School of Continuing Education at St. John's University.

The BRAIN BOOSTER

Your Guide to Rapid Learning and Remembering

ROBERT W. FINKEL

A SPECTRUM BOOK

Prentice-Hall, Inc., Englewood Cliffs, New Jersey 07632

Library of Congress Cataloging in Publication Data

Finkel, Robert W.
   The brain booster.

   "A Spectrum book"--T.p. verso.
   Includes index.
   1. Mnemonics. 2. Learning, Psychology of. I. Title.
BF385.F54 1983   153.1   83-17642
ISBN 0-13-080895-4
ISBN 0-13-080887-3 (pbk.)

Lovingly Dedicated to Carla

This book is available at a special discount when ordered in bulk quantities. Contact Prentice-Hall, Inc., General Publishing Division, Special Sales, Englewood Cliffs, N.J. 07632.

10 9 8 7 6 5 4 3 2 1

Printed in the United States of America

ISBN 0-13-080895-4

ISBN 0-13-080887-3 {PBK.}

Prentice-Hall International, Inc., *London*
Prentice-Hall of Australia Pty. Limited, *Sydney*
Prentice-Hall of Canada Inc., *Toronto*
Prentice-Hall of India Private Limited, *New Delhi*
Prentice-Hall of Japan, Inc., *Tokyo*
Prentice-Hall of Southeast Asia Pte. Ltd., *Singapore*
Whitehall Books Limited, *Wellington, New Zealand*
Editora Prentice-Hall do Brasil Ltda., *Rio de Janeiro*

CONTENTS

ACKNOWLEDGMENTS AND CREDITS

We are pleased to credit the following sources of reprinted material:

Excerpts from A. R. Luria, *The Mind of a Mnemonist*. Translated from the Russian by Lynn Solotaroff. © 1968 by Basic Books, Inc. By permission of Basic Books, Inc. and by Jonathon Cape Ltd.

Quotation from Dale Carnegie, *How to Win Friends and Influence People*. © 1964 by Dorothy Carnegie. By permission of Simon and Schuster.

Drawing of skull from Langley, Telford, and Chistensen, *Dynamic Anatomy and Physiology*. © 1974 by McGraw-Hill. Reprinted by permission.

Diagram of nuclear reactor from Robert S. Rouse and Robert O. Smith, *Energy: Resource, Slave, Pollutant: A Physical Science Text*. © 1975 by Macmillan Publishing Co., Inc. Reprinted by permission.

Article by Mitchel L. Zoler, *Touch, Taste, and the Desire to Eat*. This material originally appeared in *Science Digest*, April, 1981. Reprinted by permission of the author.

Excerpt on the development of language and speech from Gloria J. Borden and Katherine S. Harris, *Speech Science Primer*. © 1980 by the Williams and Wilkins Co., Baltimore. Reprinted by permission.

The readings "Character and Characterization" and "Plot" from Oscar G. Brockett, *The Essential Theater*. © 1980 by Holt, Rinehart and Winston. Reprinted by permission.

The article on "The Black Death" is extracted from the *Man-Made World* published by McGraw-Hill, © 1971 by Polytechnic Institute of Brooklyn. Reprint publication of this article is not an endorsement by the original copyright owner.

Excerpts from an article by W. Langer, *The Black Death*. This originally appeared in *Scientific American*, February, 1964. By permission of W. H. Freeman and Company.

Excerpt from an article by Timothy Ferris, *Physics' Newest Frontier*. This originally appeared in *New York Times Magazine*, Sept. 26, 1982. © 1982 by The New York Times Company. Reprinted by permission.

Excerpts from *Intelligence Can Be Taught* by Arthur Whimbey with Linda S. Whimbey. © 1975 by Arthur Whimbey and published by E. P. Dutton & Co. Reprinted by permission.

We are especially thankful to the International Paper Company for permission to reprint articles from the "Power of the Printed Word" program: *How to Read an Annual Report* by Jane Bryant Quinn; *How to Write a Resume* by Jerrold G. Simon, Ed.D.; *How to Write With Style* by Kurt Vonnegut; and *How to Write a Business Letter* by Malcomb Forbes.

Special thanks to Mrs. Lillian Connolly for her wholehearted help in typing and preparing the manuscript.

I am grateful to my dear wife, Carla, for her careful and constructive reading of the manuscript and for making everything worthwhile.

ABOUT THIS
UNIQUE BOOK

This is a book of practical techniques for learning and remembering. It shows you how to learn more, faster—with clear, lasting recall. You can acquire the techniques easily and quickly and use them immediately for your studies, interests, or profession.

Studies in brain physiology, memory, educational psychology, and a host of other cognitive sciences reveal that we have awesome mental potential—and that at best we use very little of it. Fortunately, the cognitive sciences indicate ways to reach your untapped powers to help you understand and assimilate information and ideas. This book shows you how.

The Brainbooster is your instruction manual. It will teach you to deepen your comprehension, to absorb information rapidly, to remember much more, much longer, to penetrate problems, and to become more effective in writing, teaching, and public speaking. It is richly illustrated with examples and applications and contains both how-to steps and reasons behind them.

The techniques are even more useful because they are simple and easy to learn. They work by changing your perception of information to

forms your mind can easily digest. Some techniques are ancient theatrical devices with a new respectability bestowed by the cognitive sciences. Others are related to the practices of various expert thinkers such
as mnemonists, problem solvers, scientists, and other intellectual athletes.

This is the first book to bring together so many learning techniques
and applications. It is unique in explaining how the diverse techniques
arise from their common roots—a few basic elements like the telescopic
approach and method of substitute images. Moreover, these elements
are derived from basic scientific findings or well-tested practice and
experience.

Many of the techniques are presented for the first time: the
telescopic approach to organization, the S.O.S. technique for problem
solving, the method for mental recording of lectures and films, and the
technique of animated digits for remembering numbers. These techniques draw upon—or distill—common practices used by experts.

A special feature of the central techniques presented in the book is
that they can be used immediately, usually after one sitting. The original
versions of many powerful techniques required much practice to master, which no doubt limited the use of learning techniques in education. The new techniques make it easier to learn how to learn.

The Brainbooster guides you step by step. It shows you the
memory systems of great mnemonists: how to remember words, terms,
and foreign vocabularies; recall a dozen people after a single introduction; retain telephone numbers, dates, prices, and numbers of any
length. And these techniques are joined with principles of mental
organization to create rapid learning techniques: how to learn diagrams,
processes, and facts; read deeply and remember readings in graphic
detail; improve writing, teaching, and speech making; solve problems;
absorb lectures, presentations, and films, even without notes—and
more. There are clear, useful discussions of brain function, the mechanisms of memory, and nutrients which boost memory and intelligence.
Best of all, this book shows you can enjoy learning quickly and easily.

ABOUT TECHNIQUES

1

Simple, easily learned techniques
of organization, visualization, and association

Joan Conte is the most successful premedical student in her college. During her class in organic chemistry, the other students take notes feverishly. The whir of tape recorders blends with the professor's monotone, and chemical hieroglyphics cover the blackboard. After the lecture Joan holds court in the student lounge where, without a textbook or notes, she recreates and interprets the lecture, even drawing complex chemical structures from memory. The other students usually take hours of additional study to approach Joan's mastery of the material.

A young executive, Bart Welkson, wanted an important position in a New York concern. His chances seemed poor because he was competing with more experienced people. After a long wait, Bart received a ninety-page company report and an invitation to be interviewed by the firm's executive board on the following day. The company vice-president apologized at the interview for not sending the report early enough for a close examination. Bart replied that he had fully digested the report—just mention any page number at random, and, without looking, he would describe the contents and offer his thoughts about them. The interviewers took the bait, and Bart verified his claim, page after page. The astonished board members offered him the position before he left the room.

Such feats of learning and remembering appear virtually superhuman, but Joan and Bart are very much like you and me. They were not born with this exceptional ability—they developed it. And you can, too.

THE CHARACTERISTICS OF LEARNING TECHNIQUES

Your learning abilities can soar with simple techniques of organization, visualization, and association. These are not traditional study methods or exercises in willpower and determination, but far more effective measures that are easily learned and that can be applied immediately to your studies or work.

This seems incredible to people who believe that the ability to learn is a fixed inherited trait and that only hard work, attention, and discipline can make a difference in how quickly or thoroughly we learn. Such attitudes are widespread, although they are discredited by research in psychology and education and by everyday experience. Factors such as cultural background, format of presentation, interest in the subject matter, personality, and even humor have significant impacts on learning. Perhaps it is not surprising, then, that techniques which organize and improve your perception of information can and do increase comprehension and memory.

A learning technique is a procedure for organizing or interpreting information to improve understanding or recall. For example, a map may be learned by mentally shifting its elements into an easily recognized pattern. The actual map is then remembered as a perturbation of the simplified map. A more familiar technique is to form acronyms—the word HOMES reminds us of the great lakes (Huron, Ontario, Michigan, Erie, and Superior). Still another technique is identifying topic sentences to improve reading comprehension. All these are useful aids to learning and are restricted forms of the more fundamental and widely applicable techniques presented in this book.

WHY TECHNIQUES WORK

We are told that we use only a miniscule fraction of our mental capabilities. How can we have such enormous potential and realize so little of it? Why are we unable to learn much more, much faster, despite our best efforts?

These questions invite speculation. I think that most of the information in "book learning" is in a form not easily grasped and retained by our brains—brains that are best designed for more fundamental or primitive functions. For example, our verbal memory is less powerful than our primordial visual memory. I suspect that the spectacular success of learning techniques is partly due to their encoding of information into forms found most "digestible" by the brain.

As you use learning techniques, you will find yourself rendering information digestible through vivid visualization, association, and organization. Visualization is employed to tap the powerful visual memory mechanism. Association links old and new information in a manner we seem neurologically well suited to absorb. And, perhaps most important, well-organized material is easily understood and easily recalled.

Another reason for the effectiveness of learning techniques is that they create a state of attentiveness in the learner. When you use learning techniques, you interact with the material. This is a creative, interesting process which fosters high levels of concentration.

SOURCES OF LEARNING TECHNIQUES

Technological leaps are commonplace in the modern world. Television reaches around the earth, robots run our factories, we probe outer space, conquer myriad diseases, and increase life expectancy. Advances in sports physiology enable a new generation of champions to topple record after record. How incongruous it is that the usual advice we receive for learning in the space age amounts to "pay attention, rehearse often, and try hard."

We do know how to improve learning ability. Recent findings in brain physiology, nutrition, educational psychology, and memory research all suggest applications which can improve your ability to learn. Moreover, we have a great legacy of learning techniques; they are practiced regularly by various professionals. People with trained memories, mnemonists, easily recall hundreds of items in minutes. Engineers and physical scientists "read" equations and crack problems with a barrage of techniques. Many artists paint complex and detailed scenes without having the subject in view. Some public speakers lecture at length without notes. Seasoned specialists of all kinds devour dense reports in their fields quickly and easily.

These impressive skills are "tricks of the trade" that are usually not taught formally, but which are learned by experience and observation. Although they are very diverse, they are all products of mental organization, visualization, and association—the common denominators of learning techniques.

I have unabashedly borrowed, altered, and developed learning techniques from all these sources. Some techniques, then, are based on scientific findings, and others are rooted in experience and practice. I have distilled the techniques to a few that are most effective and most easily mastered.

ON READING THIS BOOK

The chapters of this book fit into one of three categories: (1) central techniques that have the widest utility; (2) special applications of these central techniques (sometimes including peripheral techniques); and (3) general information. The application chapters are not essential to the rest of the book. Of course, the more you read, the better for your mastering learning techniques. But do not feel compelled to read chapters that hold little interest for you. A student might omit the chapter on remembering names and faces, whereas a businessperson might happily ignore the chapter on chemical structures. Short summaries are included for all the central technique chapters and for a few unspecialized application chapters.

A majority of the chapters include examples and exercises. I strongly recommend that you work through these. It will require some effort, but the reward is an ability to learn more, faster, and more thoroughly.

2
QUESTIONS
AND ANSWERS

Most frequently asked
questions about the techniques

I demonstrate techniques to audiences by helping them learn a map of an industrial park. Minutes after seeing how to expand their thinking, the participants give directions from any particular building to any other—without looking at the map. They are amused and rightfully impressed by their own powers.

As a climax to the demonstration, I distribute copies of a current news magazine like *Time* or *Newsweek* (or an annual report, for a business audience). People then call out random page numbers, and I summarize the articles on these pages from memory, describing even the photographs and layouts.

The demonstration is followed by a question period, and the following questions are based on these sessions. Many of the points raised here are discussed throughout the book, but it is useful to anticipate these questions now.

Q: **Do you have a "trick" memory?**
A: I have a normal memory, probably much like yours. I often cannot remember where I parked my car, and I forget my own telephone number—maybe this qualifies as a trick memory!

Q: **Is this primarily a memory improvement course?**

Memory techniques are an important part of this subject, but we are most concerned with learning in general. This includes cognitive and conceptual skills as well as memory: how to extract ideas from reading and listening, how to solve problems, how to take notes, and how to organize thoughts are all addressed.

The memory aspects are certainly the most showy and impressive. After all, you cannot demonstrate learning without also demonstrating memory. Techniques that specifically assist memory are called *mnemonics* or *mnemonic devices.* I used several of these to remember the demonstration magazine.

Incidentally, I did not memorize the demonstration magazine word for word as you might memorize a poem or a script. I prefer to say that I *learned* it, insofar as I know the central points and recall the most important details. Nevertheless, the demonstration is always seen as a memory feat.

Q: **Will I be able to learn an entire magazine by page number?**
A: Yes. It involves nothing more than an application of several techniques. Professional mnemonists do similar things for theatrical impact on stage.

Q: **What is the quality of this kind of learning? How long will it be remembered?**
A: No doubt you fear that learning with techniques is so easy that somehow the quality of learning must be inferior. Perhaps it is rapidly forgotten or easily confused.

The opposite is true. You will probably remember the demonstration map for weeks, although I can hardly imagine a more useless bit of information. The bold impressions made with techniques persist longer and more clearly than memories achieved though rote.

Q: **Are the techniques based on willpower or positive thinking?**
A: No. The techniques are based on principles of organization, visualization, and association. When you use techniques, you are improving your view of information so that it is easier to understand and easier to remember.

Q: **My time is very limited. How long will it take before I can use the techniques?**
A: These techniques can be used immediately. The time you invest is the time you spend reading the book or participating in the seminar.

Of course, you greatly improve your learning skills as you use them. You can practice on material you would otherwise learn by standard means. Usually, learning with a new technique will be as fast or faster than the conventional approach, even in the first application.

There are several powerful learning techniques that require considerable practice before they can be used. In the case of each of these I have found an alternative that is equally useful for rapid learning, but which can be used immediately.

Q: **What subjects are suitable for rapid learning techniques?**
A: Learning can be accelerated in most subjects. Techniques are effective for reading, listening, taking notes, solving problems, and the recall of facts, terms, and numbers. These are certainly important skills for a majority of subject areas.

Naturally, the usefulness of the techniques varies with the subjects or topics. There are some topics that elude the application of techniques. For instance, I don't yet have good suggestions for treating foreign grammars, although techniques work nicely for foreign vocabulary.

Q: **I am a teacher. Can learning techniques be used to improve instruction?**
A: Yes. A number of rapid learners use techniques in the classroom with exceptional success. A chapter on teaching with techniques is included in the book.

Q: **Will this course make me more intelligent?**
A: I think so, although some people disagree. They regard intelligence as inflexibly fixed by genetics, and they describe it with a single number, the I.Q. If this view is realistic, no amount of learning and no mental skill you develop—however extraordinary—has the smallest effect on your intelligence.

You and I recognize intelligence when we see it: the abilities to learn, to create, to think through problems, to understand concepts, to remember, and so on. And most of these attributes can be improved with techniques.

Q: **Is speed reading taught in this seminar?**
A: I treat the most basic techniques for rapid reading. My main emphasis, however, is reading for better learning.

Q: **What is the level of instruction?**
A: Most of the information is aimed at the level of the reading public, which I assume to be bright, but unfamiliar with any learning techniques.

Q: **Do the techniques become habitual? Do you use them all the time?**
A: No. You need to make a conscious effort to apply most of the techniques. Everyday reading and listening usually don't warrant this effort. You can "switch on" techniques whenever the demands to learn and remember become pressing.

Many former students and clients report that they went through a long period during which they mixed the techniques with their old study methods. This is a very good procedure, because a lot of mental energy is spent in applying new techniques. Mixing new and old methods gives you time to become comfortable and confident with the new techniques. You don't give up common sense just because you learn some powerful techniques.

Q: **Is any special ability required?**
A: No. Normal individuals learn most or all of the techniques without diffi-

culty. Only rarely does someone claim to be unable to visualize events or to organize certain material. Some very bright people with learning disabilities also have trouble using several of the techniques. But these are exceptions.

Most people are quite unaware that they have immense intellectual potential. The role of technique is to enable you to realize some of your latent powers.

3

YOUR MIND'S EYE

Two central memory techniques:
the memory chain and substitute images

In the next few minutes you will learn how to memorize long lists after reading them just once! You will use a *memory chain* method based upon principles of visualization and association. This technique and the related *substitute images* technique are the foundation for most memory courses and exhibitions.

THE MEMORY CHAIN

A memory chain is a device for memorizing a sequence of items. The idea is to have the first item remind you of the second, the second remind you of the third, and so on through the list. You can do this easily by creating striking mental images that link each new item to the last item.

The technique is demonstrated on the following list. Please resist the temptation to memorize the list without reading the instructions. This would just waste your energy and prove nothing. Instead, follow the instructions next to each item and work your way down the list. Don't hurry, but don't stop to rehearse either.

Item	Instructions
egg	Imagine a huge egg.
shoe	To associate *shoe* with *egg*, imagine an animated shoe kicking a hole in the egg. Visualize this clearly for a moment or two.
car	Link *car* with *shoe* by imagining that the shoe grows into a car and develops headlights and wheels. Don't be deterred by the absurdity of the image: see it clearly and move to the new item.
tree	Associate *tree* by visualizing a tree sprouting from the hood of a car.
frankfurter	Continue on your own by making any fantastic association to connect *frankfurter* with *tree*. Visualize this clearly.
apple	Continue on your own. Make the association unusual. Visualize it clearly and go on.
cigar	Continue on your own. Trust yourself—do not rehearse earlier associations.
flower	Continue on your own. It is most important to visualize your association for a moment.
chair	Continue on your own. Almost any bizarre association will do, if you can visualize it.
desk	"Ah," you say, *desk* and *chair* are naturally associated, so this will be easy to remember. Not so. It is easier to remember items that have unusual associations (like *tree* and *frankfurter*). Use your imagination to distort the relation between desk and chair (for example, by exaggerating the size of one).
chalk	Continue on your own.
watch	Continue on your own.

Now repeat the entire list from memory—then repeat it backward!

SOME FEATURES OF THE TECHNIQUE

Very likely you are impressed by your ability to remember the list so easily and accurately. Your associations gave meaning to the list, and your visualizations made the associations memorable and vivid. The memory chain technique uses your natural abilities to learn by association and visualization rather than by plodding repetition. Your creativity and imagination replace deadening drill.

Despite these facts, people usually ask me how long they will remember a list that was learned in such an "artificial" manner (implying that learning by rote is "natural"). You may expect to remember the list for days or even weeks without conscious rehearsal. In any event, you will remember it much longer than if you had learned it by rote.

Associations are most effective when they are imaginative and unusual. A tree bearing hot dog "fruit" and a shoe sporting headlights are easily remembered. Many people are uncomfortable using these silly associations. They feel that frivolous thoughts are undignified, even though they are completely private. If you are one of the few people who cannot overcome this attitude, you can still imagine less dramatic or silly associations, but they will require somewhat more attention and rehearsal.

You can form strong associations by imposing one or more of the following features:

1. Unusual sizes or numbers (for example, a huge egg or hundreds of tiny apples).
2. Unusual materials (for example, a bird made of bricks or wheels made of watches).
3. Dynamic motion, including growth, sex, or violence (for example, a shoe kicking an egg).

The first item in a list should be particularly outstanding because it has no prior association.

The memory chain technique requires that you visualize an association clearly before you continue to the next item. This is the most important step in forming a memory chain—you must picture the association.

Now you can form a memory chain for another list. You'll see that your own associations are the most effective. Once you have pictured an association vividly, trust your memory and continue to the next association. Even when you form a memory chain slowly, you are memorizing many times faster than you possibly can without a technique.

Exercise

Memorize the following list using the memory chain technique.

foot	book	eyeglasses
wall	matches	frying pan
dog	tire	candle
key	carrot	nose

A MAN WITH A BOUNDLESS MEMORY

One of the greatest memories ever documented belonged to a Russian newspaper reporter, Solomon Veniaminovich Sheresheveskii. Experiments showed that he had no difficulty reproducing word series and number sequences of any length. Although he memorized hundreds of thousands of series, Sheresheveskii could recall them upon request fifteen or sixteen years later. His memory had no apparent limits, either in its capacity or in its permanence.

In the mid 1920s Sheresheveskii was nearly thirty, but still unaware that he was in any way unusual—doesn't everyone remember everything they are told? The puzzled reporter was sent by his editor to a psychology laboratory for testing. There he stunned the renowned psychologist A. R. Luria, who began a study of Sheresheveskii that lasted nearly thirty years.

Professor Luria's report shows that Sheresheveskii's titanic memory was due primarily to his *vivid visual imagery* and *graphic associations;* the very same mechanisms you use in this chapter.

Sheresheveskii did not set out to master concrete visualization and association—mastery was forced upon him by a mental quirk. He *had* to visualize every thought in concrete and specific images. His inner world was one of myriad particulars, each with an isolated existence, without patterns, relationships, or generalizations. He said he could only understand what he could visualize.

This strange quirk, which was responsible for his great gift, also placed great limitations on him. Sheresheveskii was unable to understand abstractions like "nothing" and "infinity." He had to memorize a predictable sequence of digits with the same concentration he needed for a random number list. He even had great difficulty recognizing people's faces because, as he described:

> They're so changeable. A person's expression depends on his mood and on the circumstances under which you happen to meet him. People's faces are constantly changing; it's the different shades of expression that confuse me and make it so hard to remember faces.*

Sometime after Shereshevskii became aware of his powers he brought them to the stage and became a professional mnemonist. He deliberately refined and developed his techniques to make them error-free and to enable himself to handle any type of nonsense sequences or passages in unfamiliar foreign languages. He was successful and became quite well known.

A major difference between you and Shereshevskii is that you have the option to use memory devices, whereas he simply had no choice. There are professional mnemonists today who are free of mental aberrations but who can rival his performances. However, unlike Shereshevskii, these talented individuals are unlikely to remember trivia forever. Their healthy minds organize information, retaining what seems important and eliminating the mental junk.

This is not the full story of the man-who-remembered-everything. You will have several occasions to learn more about the art of remembering from his case history.

SUBSTITUTE IMAGES

By now you recognize that your ability to remember long lists of objects is impressive but not very useful. Most of the words, terms, or ideas you want to remember are not visual descriptions. Nevertheless, your technique for remembering objects can be upgraded to help you remember verbal information: simply create mental images that remind you of the original wording.

---

*From *The Mind of A Mnemonist* by A. R. Luria. Translated from the Russian by Lynn Solotaroff. © 1968 by Basic Books, Inc. By permission of Basic Books, Inc. and Jonathan Cape Limited.

This technique of substituting graphic images to represent abstract words was essential to mnemonist Shereshevskii's thinking. When he heard the word *green,* he imagined a green flowerpot; *America* was represented by an image of Uncle Sam; and the word *transcendent* evoked a picture of his teacher looking at a monument. These concrete images served as cues to recall the original words.

You can easily develop this substitute image technique. Suppose, for example, that a student of political science is to be tested on the basic statistics of several countries. In order to structure the essay answers, the student wants to remember the list of key words given below. Put yourself in the student's situation and follow the instructions next to each word—you will have ample opportunity to create your own imagery later. Use bold, clear, exaggerated images and spend about thirty or forty seconds on each word.

Words	*Instructions*
location	Imagine an arrow embedded in some *location* on a map. Pay special attention to this image because it begins the sequence.
area (square kilometers)	A square was the first area you studied in school. Visualize a paper square attached like a flag to the arrow. The square represents *area.*
population	Picture hundreds of tiny people emerging from the square. The people represent *population.*
chief cities	The people pour into a city building (representing *cities*) until the building walls bulge. If you think you may need a reminder for *chief,* put a huge fire chief hat on top of the building.
government	Use a crown as a symbol for government, and continue on your own by making a very graphic association with the city building.
manufacturing	Continue on your own by imagining any particular manufactured item: if you decide that it will represent *manufacturing,* it will work. Make a strong link into the crown and proceed.

agriculture	Continue on your own. Use specific items, not a vague scene.
raw materials	Continue on your own.
monetary unit	Continue on your own.

Finally, repeat the list from memory.

SENSE IMPRESSIONS

Educators tell us to involve as many senses as possible when we are studying. When learning new terms, for instance, it helps to hear the term, to speak it, and to write it. It is good advice. This chapter is concerned with visual impressions, and we want to embellish these with other sensory information to make them even stronger memory aids.

Some people taste names, hear pictures, feel smells, and see dancing colors in the sound of a voice. A rare disorder called *synesthesia* includes these and other blurrings between the borders of the senses. Sheresheveskii had such marked synesthesia that he "saw" words and sounds as puffs of steam, animated colored strips, and the like. Professor Luria was not thinking of the most powerful memory in the world when he asked whether Sheresheveskii could find his way home from a testing center. The reply shows the blitz of sensations the mnemonist lived with:

> Come now, how could I possibly forget. After all here is this fence, it has such a salty taste and feels so rough; furthermore it has such a sharp piercing sound. . . .*

Sheresheveskii's synesthesia and his bottomless memory were related. The possibility that both extremely rare conditions occurred independently in the same individual is too remote. Certainly the Russian's visualizations were so bold, so saturated with impressions from every sense, that they were etched deeply in his mind.

This is a way to amplify your own impressions. Dress your mental images with imagined tastes, colors, textures, and sounds. The bolder,

*Ibid.

the better. After all, the most important step in memory systems is to form vivid images—and various sensory cues intensify them. No one can forget a salty-tasting, rough, shrill fence.

SUMMARY

Memory Chain: To remember a list, associate the first item with the second, the second with the third, and so on. Associations are most effective when they are imaginative and unusual. Items of unusual size, unusual material, or having dynamic motion are best remembered. Visualization is the most important step in forming a memory chain; picture each association clearly before continuing to the next item.

Substitute Images: To remember words, create concrete images to serve as cues. Your "natural" memory cements the word to the image, however abstract the word may be.

Sense Impressions: Embellish visual images with tastes, colors, textures, and sounds. These make images more vivid and memorable.

Exercises

1. Memorize the following list using the memory chain and substitute image techniques.

tea	noise	baseball
arm	fish	flavor
friendship	horn	planet
candle	wonderful	cash register

2. As you will see in later chapters, one of the most useful applications of memory chain and substitute image techniques is to memorize *key words*. The key words are reminders of facts and ideas. The list of key words in this exercise should remind you of the central points narrated about Shereshevskii in this chapter. Memorize the list and see if you remember the associated ideas. (Don't bother to remember the ideas word by word.)

Key Words	*Fact or Idea*
reporter	Shereshevskii was a newspaper reporter when his powers were discovered.
no limits	His memory was limitless in capacity and duration.
experiments	He was the subject of psychological experiments for nearly thirty years.
techniques	Shereshevskii used visualization and association.
disorder	He had a disorder that forced him to use imagery.
professional	He became a professional performer of memory feats.
substitute images	Shereshevskii used concrete images as cues for words.

4
APPLICATION: REMEMBERING PEOPLE

Substitute images
for remembered names and faces

An ability to remember people is a tremendous asset in business and social life. It is a skill you can master.

The famous mnemonist Harry Lorayne routinely memorizes the names of hundreds of people in an audience! He tells of his early career as a magician, when he had to demonstrate his public appeal to a potential television sponsor. Lorayne was told to perform throughout the sponsor's offices so the employees could render a verdict. It was a disastrous day for illusions as trick after trick flopped. Fortunately, Lorayne knew the power of remembering people—he learned the names of all the employees and spoke to each one. His new friends overlooked the flaws in his performance and gave him a rave review.

Dale Carnegie asserted that people have a fundamental need for recognition and appreciation. His book *How to Win Friends and Influence People* carried the message in seventeen editions within the first few months of its publication in 1937. Carnegie taught that a key to success is to give people the attention and approval they crave. This includes remembering and using the other person's name because "a man's name is to him the sweetest and most important sound in any language."*

Some detractors think this approach is cynical and simplistic, but I have not heard it criticized for failing to work. Surely it is not so malevolent to foster an interest in others and to look for something praiseworthy in them. And, after all, the truth is not less valuable for being simple.

THE BASIC IDEA

Mrs. Bump has a bump on her nose, and Mr. Longfellow is extremely tall and thin. You remember these people easily because they are described by their names. Although most names are not such descriptive labels, your imagination can make them so.

For example, Mr. Fox may have perfectly regular features, but you can imagine him with large canine ears and a long, foxlike snout. Ms. Smith can be imagined carrying a blacksmith's anvil. The name *Warnke* sounds like *worn key,* an easily visualized object. You can associate Mr. Warnke with his name simply by imagining a worn key projecting from his hair or nose or any prominent feature. These examples illustrate the technique for remembering names: create an image that reminds you of the name and associate the image with the person.

Use this procedure to remember the names of the people in Figures 4.1 through 4.4. In each case the name sounds like something visualizable. Associate the substitute image and the person in any bizarre way. The people involved won't mind your imaginative treatment (if you don't tell them about it). After you have associated the names and faces, cover the captions, and check that you can recall the names in reverse order.

THE COMPLETE TECHNIQUE

How can you remember names that do not sound like visualizable objects? You can create substitute images that remind you of part or all of

*Reprinted by permission of Simon and Schuster, Inc.

FIGURE 4.1. Warnke

FIGURE 4.2. Lance

FIGURE 4.3. Chambers

26

FIGURE 4.4. Fox

the name. For example, *Turner* can be replaced by *turnip*, and the name *Serifin* might be approximated by *seared fin* or *surfing*. With a small effort, your natural memory will reconstruct the original name from the substitute image.

The substitute images can be simple or very complex. The names *Mary* and *Paul* might be converted to *marry* (imagine Mary in a bridal gown) and *pail* (imagine Paul with a pail on his head). You want to concentrate on the sound rather than the spelling. To remember *Veniaminovich*, you might substitute *when I am in a ditch*, and *Sheresheveskii* can be built from *share a shaver's ski*.

Most often, the match between name and image is not very close. But almost any fragments that remind you of the original sound will work. *Car* works for *Carla* or *Carl*, and *point* should be sufficient for *Poindexter*. You can simply remember to fill out the actual name from these cues.

Try this technique to associate the names and faces in Figures 4.5 through 4.8. Don't be concerned that you were "fed" some of the images, and remember that vivid imagery is the most important element in this technique. Review once, and then test yourself by covering the captions.

FIGURE 4.5. Serifin

FIGURE 4.6. Murphy

FIGURE 4.7. Turner

FIGURE 4.8. Gibson

EMBELLISHMENTS

When it is difficult to think of a substitute image with the "right" sound, a rhyme can be equally useful. Some examples: *bones* for *Jones, warts* for *Schwartz,* and *plant tin* for *Blanton.* The rhymes do not have to be very close to the name to work well.

It helps to link substitute images to a person's most outstanding feature. Robert has curly hair, so we can imagine a robber's mask protruding from his curls. Carla's big eyes may be seen as the headlights of a car. When you meet these people again, the features that first caught your attention will remind you of their names.

Use substitute imagery to remember the names and faces in Figures 4.9 through 4.12. Review once, and then test yourself by identifying all the people in Figure 4.13.

FIGURE 4.9. Blanton

FIGURE 4.10. Schwartz

FIGURE 4.11. Jones

FIGURE 4.12. Giordano

ADVICE ABOUT NAMES

Remembering names is a formidable task when you are introduced to dozens of people in a matter of minutes. A whirl of grins and handshakes usually accompanies introductions that are only half heard. If you are intent on remembering names, you must slow the introductions enough to hear the names pronounced clearly. People appreciate your interest when you ask them to repeat their names for clarification.

Even in the best circumstances, it takes time to develop adequate substitute images. At first they may take as much as a minute or two, too long for rapid introductions. Nevertheless, you can digest scores of names immediately by obtaining, in advance, a list of people that you expect to meet at a gathering. As introductions are made, simply associate the prepared images with the new faces.

FIGURE 4.13. This is a composite of all twelve photographs

5
APPLICATION: VOCABULARY, LANGUAGES, TERMINOLOGY

Substitute imagery for learning
vocabulary, terminology, and foreign languages

When memory giant Sheresheveskii took to the stage, audiences often challenged him to remember nonsensical words and phrases. Because of his learning "handicap," he was forced to convert the sounds into images. The technique he developed was to associate meaningful images with many sounds. This was so effective that, fifteen years after a single hearing of poetry in a foreign language, he was able to recall and pronounce it perfectly.

Of course, Sheresheveskii's approach required long, intense practice to develop a repertoire of symbols for every possible sound. For our purposes, this is more effort than it is worth—there are at least forty basic sounds in English. You can speed your learning of vocabulary and terminology severalfold with a much less demanding modification of his technique.

SOUNDS AND IMAGES

Perhaps the simplest way to remember unfamiliar words is to create substitute images that remind you of the sound of the original word. For example, the word *egregious* (meaning outstandingly bad) might be converted to *egg reach us*, which can be visualized. You can reconstruct the original sound with a bit of concentration.

Most often, the substitution sounds even less like the original: *tort* (meaning a wrong subject to a civil suit) can be replaced by *tart*, and *pelf* (meaning ill-gotten wealth) can be changed to *elf*. Almost any fragments of the original sounds will serve as cues. Again, the most crucial step is forming a vivid image; this is far more important than worrying how closely the substitute sound matches the original.

In many cases it helps to use substitute words that rhyme with the original words. This shifts your attention to word endings, and it may be easier to find substitutes for these. Examples: *ouch* for *avouch* and *annoyed* for *sphenoid*.

Bear in mind that forming a substitute image is part of the learning process. The time you spend creating the substitutes is not wasted. Even when the substitute seems feeble, the effort and attention you devote to the original word make a bold impression on your memory. The technique does not relieve you of the need to concentrate on the word, but it makes your efforts more productive.

Three elements are involved when you learn an unfamiliar word: sound, meaning, and spelling. In most languages it is not difficult to spell a word when it is pronounced. Of course, there are many exceptions that trip weak spellers like myself, but it is still good technique to concentrate first on sound and meaning and then to practice spelling separately.

You can link sound with meaning simply by extending your creative visualization process. For example, since *pelf* means dishonestly acquired wealth, you might visualize an elf running away with stolen money. The whole process is relatively easy to perform and can speed your learning rate for vocabulary and terminology severalfold.

APPLICATION: ENGLISH VOCABULARY

Use technique to learn the following list of vocabulary words. Treat three or four words at a time, and then review them just once before proceeding. Take your time. Even if you spend a minute or two devising a substitute image, you will be learning much faster and remembering much longer than you can by rote. Test yourself by recalling the meaning from the word and vice versa.

Word	Meaning	Suggested Imagery
egregious	outstandingly bad	*egg reach us*
defalcate	embezzle or misuse funds	*the fall cake* (Picture a cake falling apart, revealing embezzled money inside.)
mountebank	charlatan; con artist	Create your own vivid image for *mountebank*. Link this image to the meaning.
misogamy	hatred of marriage	*massage me*
hegira	flight from danger	Choose your own.
philatelist	stamp collector	*Phil ate the list*
avouch	to affirm: I will *avouch* the lawyer's integrity	Continue on your own.
panegyric	formal or public praise	Your choice.
pelf	dishonestly acquired wealth	Your choice.
threnody	a song of lament; a dirge	Your choice.
tort	a legal wrong subject to civil action	Your choice.

APPLICATION: FRENCH VOCABULARY

Some French nouns are given below in phonetic form (without articles), together with their English translations. Use the procedures of this chapter to learn the list. Test yourself by recalling the English from the French and vice versa.

English	Phonetic French	Suggested Imagery
stomach	vahntr	*vendor* (Imagine a vendor with a huge stomach.)
road	root	Choose your own image.
bed	lee	*leaf*

English	Phonetic French	Suggested Imagery
world	mohnd	Your choice.
hunter	shah-SUHR	*chaser* (one who chases) or *masseur*
cakes	gah-TOH	Your choice.
basket	pah-N'YEH	Your choice.

Whole phrases may also be treated by the substitute image technique. The phrase *comment allez-vous (how are you)* might be stretched to *come and tally you,* and a bizarre scene may be imagined to link this sound to its meaning.

APPLICATION: TERMINOLOGY

Specialists in every field have their own language. Indeed, you can learn technical terms with the same approach you used for unfamiliar or foreign vocabulary words. The word *tort,* for instance, is a legal term that was included in our English vocabulary exercise.

A slightly different problem arises when you label bones or name computer components. Here you need to identify something rather than to define it. The approach is simple enough; associate the substitute image with the thing it represents.

You can use the technique to learn parts of the facial skeleton shown in Figure 5.1. The most far-fetched and silly substitutions will work when they are vivid and visual. For example, to recall the *parietal* bone you can substitute *pear tail* and imagine a pear with a tail growing out of that part of the head. Some other substitutes can be even stranger. Look at the list of bones and substitute images on the next page.

Bone	Substitute Image
parietal	*pear tail*
coronal suture	Someone suggested *core suit* to prompt recall of both words; the image is an apple core dressed in a suit. Entirely different images arise if you know that *coronal* refers to a crown and *suture* is a stitch.
frontal	This appears so easy that you are likely to forget it due to insufficient visualization. Imagine headlights on this bone; you will not forget that it relates to the "front."
sphenoid	Try your own.
temporal	Try your own.
mastoid process	Try your own.
zygoma	Here is an imaginative one. I visualize "Brand Z" chewing gum. That is, *Z-gum*. An alternative is *sigh coma*. I leave the imagery to you.
mandible	Try your own.
mental foramen	*Foramen* applies to a small hole in the bone. Try your own images.

FIGURE 5.1.

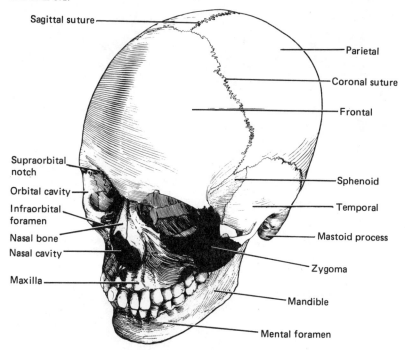

SOURCE: *Dynamic Anatomy and Physiology*, 4th Ed., Langley, Telford, and Chistensen. Fig. 5–4. © 1974, 1969, 1963, 1958 by McGraw-Hill. Reprinted by permission of McGraw-Hill Book Company.

Exercise

Memorize the facial bones labeled on the right side of the diagram. Refer to the list above for suggestions and comments. Treat three or four items at a time, and then review them just once. When you are finished, cover the labels and repeat the names in any order.

6
TELESCOPIC THINKING

Telescoping: a central
technique for organizing and learning

Years ago I watched an artist paint a portrait of an ordinary woman. I remember that portrait vividly because I saw it evolve in stages from an outline to a detailed picture.

The artist began by sketching an outline of the woman's head. He then marked the placement of her eyes, nose, and mouth. Only after the outline and basic features were formed did he begin to add details, shading, and color. As each detail came into focus, I saw how it related to the whole face. It was easy to remember new features because they were mentally associated with earlier structures.

The evolution of a portrait illustrates the *telescopic technique*—perhaps the best single method for organizing and learning difficult material. Specifically, telescoping is the technique of first treating broad outlines, followed by successive refinement of details. The approach is particularly useful for learning complex processes and lengthy or difficult texts. A number of applications are given in subsequent chapters; here I concentrate on introducing the technique and applying it to diagrams and processes.

THE BASICS OF THE TECHNIQUE

In the telescopic approach to learning, you first view gross features under low magnification. Then you increase the magnification in stages to reveal finer and finer details. The technique may also be seen as a pyramidal approach in which the most fundamental layer—the outline or the "core"—is a base for successive layers of details. Each stage or layer is clearly associated with the previous stage. When you reconstruct the outline, the details cascade forth with each layer reminding you of the next.

As an example, you can learn the blood flow relationships between the lungs, heart, and body by applying the telescopic technique. The ultimate diagram you need to understand and reproduce is shown in Figure 6.1. As usual, don't bother to see whether you can learn the diagram without techniques—you can do so easily, but your purpose is to follow the instructions closely in order to acquire the technique.

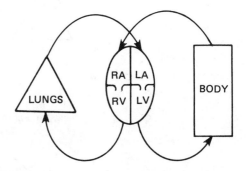

FIGURE 6.1 Circulatory System

Proceed by drawing some of the most important units in the diagram—in this case the lungs, heart, and body (Figure 6.2). This is the outline stage. Now embellish the drawing by connecting some blood vessels, say those that flow through the left side of the heart (Figure 6.3). Next, add further detail by connecting blood vessels that flow through the right side of the heart (Figure 6.4). Finally, add valves to the heart, and identify Right Atrium and Right Ventricle (RA and RV) and Left Atrium and Left Ventricle (LA and LV) as in Figure 6.5. Rehearse each stage briefly, and be sure to associate each step with the preceding stage. Then draw the complete diagram from memory.

45

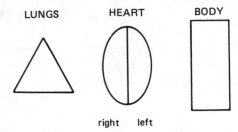

FIGURE 6.2. Three basic elements of the circulatory system: lungs, heart, and body. Notice that right and left correspond to a person facing out of the page. (We begin with the heart split vertically.)

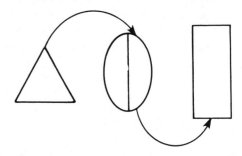

FIGURE 6.3 Fully oxygenated blood flows from the lungs to the heart. The heart pumps this blood to the body.

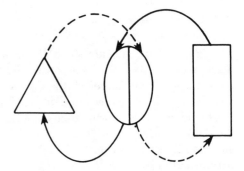

FIGURE 6.4. Blood flowing through the body surrenders its oxygen. This blood returns to the heart and is pumped to the lungs to pick up more oxygen.

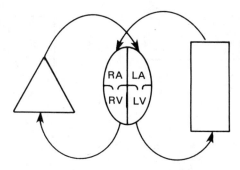

FIGURE 6.5. The heart has four chambers: left
atrium (LA), right atrium (RA), left ventricle (LV),
and right ventricle (RV).

THE REDUCTION PROCESS

In telescoping, information is packaged in layers of increasing detail.
Very often, however, the original material does not seem to have layers
which are simple enough for quick mental assimilation. You can impose
simplicity by reducing complex elements to simpler forms.

For example, a detailed diagram of the human circulatory system
would show the major blood vessels and organs. In a telescopic view
the vessels are reduced to mere lines, and organs are reduced to simple
geometric figures (as in the case of lungs and heart above). The
purpose of reducing these elements to the barest outlines is that they are
thus easily visualized and remembered.

There is no single "correct" way of choosing the elements that will
be the outline or of picking the order of adding details. You will have to
make these decisions with each new case. Nevertheless, organizing the
layers is the most important step in the process—do it carefully. You will
be learning the material as you plan your attack.

Maps, photographs, and charts can usually be made far less bewil-
dering simply by rearranging their elements into easily remembered
patterns. In the next quarter-hour or so, you can learn the campus map
shown in Figure 6.6 well enough to name the buildings and to give
directions from any building to any other without looking at the map. I
urge you to do this example because it gathers all the basic techniques
we've used to date. Let yourself be led through this case—you can treat
another map unassisted (in an exercise) at the end of the chapter.

47

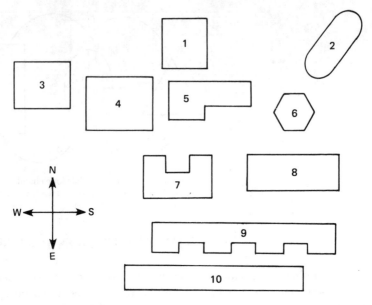

FIGURE 6.6

The first step is to reduce the original map to an outline and layers of detail that can be remembered. This process is illustrated in Figures 6.7 through 6.9. Follow the reduction so that you will be able to sketch Figure 6.9 as follows:

FIGURE 6.7.

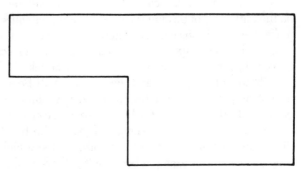

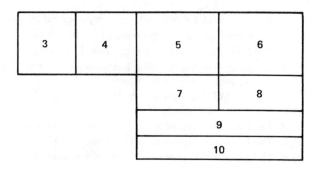

FIGURE 6.8.

1. Remember the outline in Figure 6.7.
2. Remember the first level of detail—the sectioning shown in Figure 6.8. (This may also be seen as two equal levels of detail, one for buildings 3 through 6 and another for buildings 7 through 10.)
3. Remember the second level of detail—the placement of the odd buildings 1 and 2 in Figure 6.9.

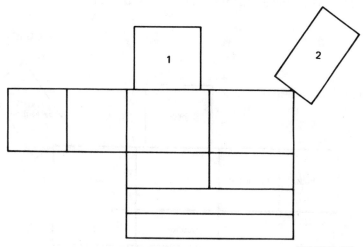

FIGURE 6.9.

Check that you can reconstruct Figure 6.9 from memory.
Now choose a substitute image to remind you of each building name:

1. The *Student Activities* building is represented by a mug of beer.
2. The *Gym* building is represented by a basketball.
3. The *Education* building is represented by chalk.
4. The *Administration* building is represented by the University President in long robes and a mortarboard.
5. The *Law* building is represented by a judge's gavel (a more dynamic image than scales of justice).
6. The *Business* building is represented by a dollar bill.
7. The *Library* is represented by a book.
8. The *Theater* is represented by a mask of comedy.
9. The *Science* building is represented by a human-sized laboratory rat.
10. The *Dormitory* is represented by a bed.

Make vivid associations and be sure that you can identify each building name from the images in Figure 6.10.

Finally, link the images together with an absurd memory chain (the only new element here is that this is a *branched list*). Begin with "chalk" on the left, and imagine that the chalk writes on the president's clothes. This enrages the president, who seizes the gavel and smashes

FIGURE 6.10.

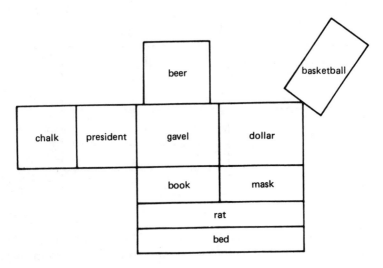

the dollar bill (to the right) and the book (below). The librarian is so upset that she disguises herself with the mask (to her right) and rides away on the giant rat (below her). The rat runs to the dormitory and goes to bed. As an afterthought, we remember the placement of the beer and the basketball by imagining beer dripping on the gavel below and a dollar bill growing out of the basketball. Look at Figure 6.10 and visualize the nonsense clearly.

When you've completed these steps, cover the diagrams and answer these questions:

1. Which building is furthest west on campus? Furthest south? Furthest east?
2. Which building is immediately east of the Education building?
3. In what direction should you go from the Administration building to reach the Law building?
4. In what direction should you go from the Law building to reach the Library? To reach the Business building? To reach the Student Activities building?
5. In what direction should you go from the Law building to reach the Science building?
6. In what direction should you go from the Theater to reach the Library? To reach the Business building?

SUMMARY

Telescoping: Telescoping is a technique whereby you first learn a broad outline, followed by successive layers of details.

Reduction Process: Identify elements that seem most significant, and reduce these to a simple visualizable pattern. This constitutes your outline. Memorize it. If you cannot decide which elements are "most significant," choose a few arbitrary elements. Your outline should be easy to visualize and recall, so do not begin with too many elements or overly complex geometric forms.

Details: Choose a level of details, preferably the most significant details, and remember these by linking them to the outline with vivid visual associations. Details may be any features you need to know, including labels, equations, and explanations. Repeat the process of adding layers of detail until the work is complete. Each layer should be strongly associated with the parts you have already treated.

Exercises

Your objective in the following exercises is to systematically apply the procedures of the above summary.

1. Figure 6.11 shows a nuclear reactor plant (old design). When the control rods are positioned as shown (not meshed with the fuel rods), nuclear reactions occur that heat water in the boiler. Steam drives the turbine and is then cooled to liquid water in the condenser, from which the water is pumped back to the boiler. The mechanical energy of the turbine is converted to electrical energy by the generator. Sketch the diagram from memory, describe the process, and identify the components.

FIGURE 6.11.

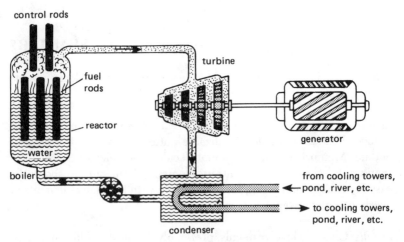

From *Energy: Resource, Slave, Pollutant,* Rouse and Smith. Copyright © by Macmillan Publishing Co., Inc. Reprinted by permission of the publisher.

2. A map of an industrial park is shown in Figure 6.12. Use telescoping to remember the map in sufficient detail to be able to tell, for any given building, the immediate neighboring buildings to the north, south, east, and west. (Reduce the map as shown in the text, and link the names of the buildings in a branched list.)

FIGURE 6.12.

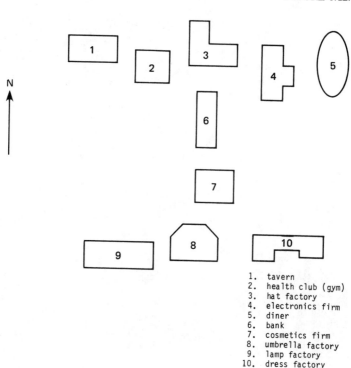

1. tavern
2. health club (gym)
3. hat factory
4. electronics firm
5. diner
6. bank
7. cosmetics firm
8. umbrella factory
9. lamp factory
10. dress factory

7

APPLICATION: CHEMICAL STRUCTURES

Telescopic techniques for
learning amino acid structures in minutes

Some biologists say that DNA molecules are life's most basic chemicals. After all, genetic messages of unimaginable antiquity are written in DNA—the blueprints of the living cell. Other students of nature see energy transformations as the pivotal activity of life. They naturally revere ATP, the energy-laden molecules that drive biological reactions. Still others, like myself, hold the romantic notion that enzymes are life's central chemicals.

Of course, life does not reside in individual molecules. It is their organization and their orchestration that somehow plays life's song. Here enzymes are the players, the conductor, and the music. Enzymes are produced from DNA instructions and are fueled by ATP, but it is the enzymes that conduct the main business of life:

Q. What chemicals extract energy and material from nutrients?
A. Enzymes.

Q. What chemicals are produced from this energy and material?
A. Enzymes.

Q. What chemicals control and regulate this production of enzymes?
A. Enzymes.

Much as English words are chains of various combinations of twenty-six letters, enzymes are chains of various combinations of twenty-odd chemical units called *amino acids*. College biology students are routinely required to learn the names and structures of these amino acids. In this chapter you will apply techniques to learn seven of these, and the approach can be extended to learning any complex chemical diagrams.

BACKGROUND

The atoms that occur most frequently in amino acids are symbolized by H (hydrogen), O (oxygen), N (nitrogen), and C (carbon). In drawings of the chemical structures, these symbols have line segments attached to represent bonds (each bond consists of a shared pair of electrons):

$$H- \qquad -O- \qquad \overset{\diagdown}{\underset{|}{N}}\diagup \qquad -\overset{|}{\underset{|}{C}}-$$

In chemical diagrams, the atomic symbols are joined together by their bond lines. Of course, each atom must have the correct number of bonds, as shown.

Amino acids have the structure summarized in the following diagram. Here the symbol R represents any one of twenty-odd different chemical "side chains." Notice that each atom has the correct number of bonds, but O–H is written in typical shorthand notation as OH. Some amino acid structures are listed in Figure 7.1 for reference. They are the structures you will learn in this chapter.

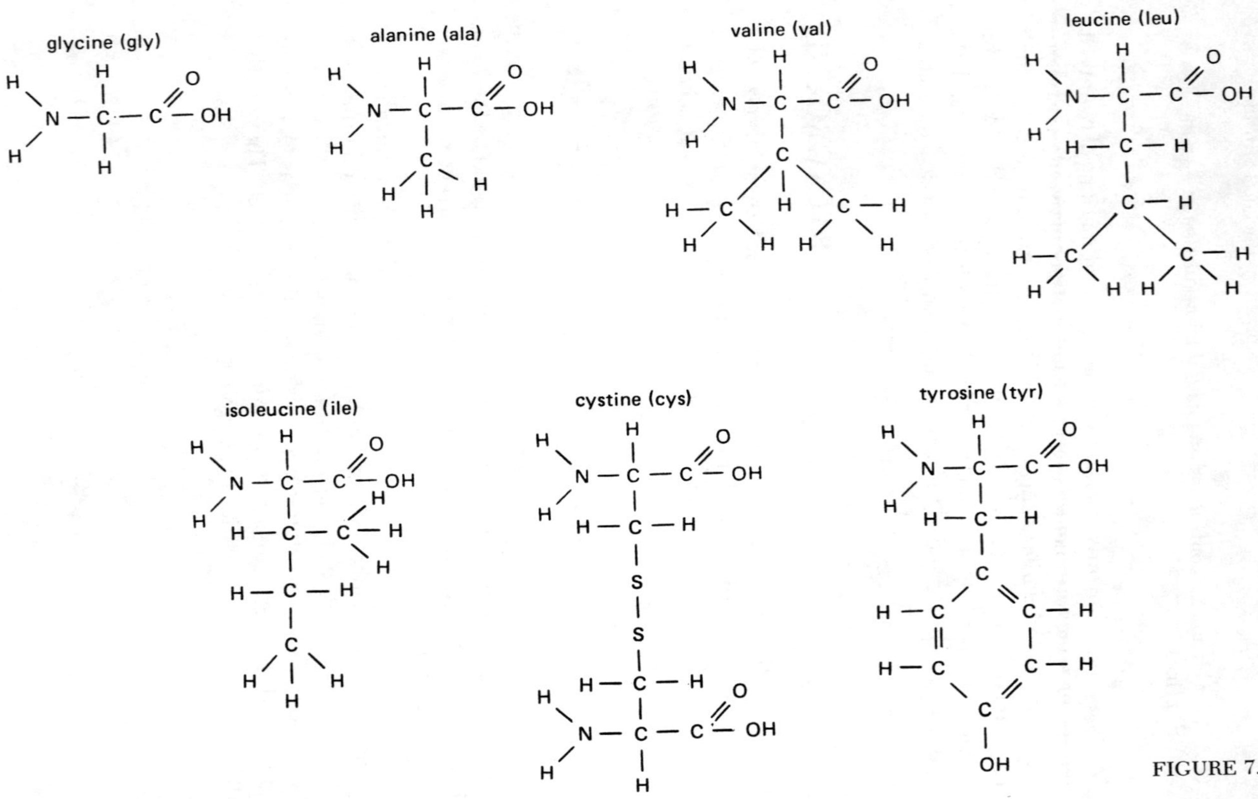

FIGURE 7.1.

58

SIMPLIFYING THE DIAGRAM

You can use telescopic and substitute image techniques to reproduce the structures from the names and vice versa. The telescopic approach requires that you first reduce the structures to a bare outline. This is the procedure: (1) Since each amino acid contains the following grouping:

$$H_2N - \overset{\overset{\displaystyle H}{|}}{C} - C \overset{\displaystyle O}{\underset{}{\diagdown}} OH$$

ignore the details of this structure and replace it with a rectangle. (2) Ignore all the confusing hydrogen atoms because they can always be added last to complete the structure. (3) Finally, reduce the next most repetitive symbol, C, to a dot. The result is shown in Figure 7.2.

FIGURE 7.2.

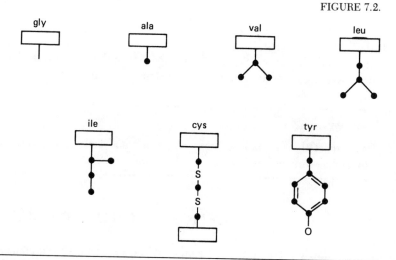

Exercise

Reconstruct the full structural diagrams for valine and leucine from their reduced diagrams (*not* from memory—that comes later). Check your results against the original diagrams.

Finally, reduce the diagrams to a still more bare outline by omitting the upper rectangles (Figure 7.3):

FIGURE 7.3.

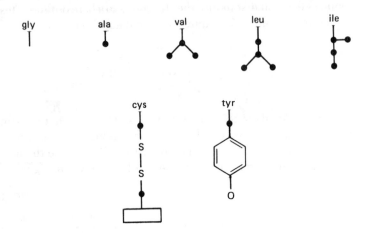

These structures are far simpler to memorize than the originals, and the successive layers of detail can be reconstructed easily.

Exercise

Reconstruct the original diagrams of glycine and isoleucine from the fully reduced diagrams (but not yet from memory).

MEMORIZING THE DIAGRAMS

You can now memorize the reduced diagrams using substitute images. For example, the word *glider* reminds me of *glycine*, so I imagine a glider with a long vertical line (representing the reduced diagram) hanging from it. The word *ale* reminds me of *alanine*, and I visualize a bottle of ale with a large dot on it. Similarly, a *veil* with three spots forming an inverted **V** is a substitute image for *valine*.

Exercises

1. Use the suggested images to recall the fully reduced diagrams for glycine, alanine, and valine.

2. Develop your own substitute images for leucine and isoleucine. Use your images to recall the fully reduced structures from the names alone. Take the time to create vivid images—even if you spend as much as three minutes on each structure, you can memorize twenty amino acids in an hour!

THE COMPLETED PROCESS

The last detail in reconstructing the originals from the reduced diagrams is to remember the characteristic "rectangle." A reduced diagram for this is

This is not pretty, but it is relatively easy to memorize. Of course, if you recognize the amine and carboxyl groups, you see this as

Amine ——●—— Carboxyl

which is a greater reduction and is easier to remember.

Exercises

1. Draw from memory the full structural diagrams for glycine, alanine, valine, leucine, and isoleucine.

2. Use the full procedure to learn cystine and tyrosine. Draw their full structures from memory.

3. Recall the amino acid names from the complete structures.

8
APPLICATION: EQUATIONS

Telescopic techniques for
reading and remembering equations

Equations are doors to knowledge and discovery, instruments of power, objects of transcendent beauty. Some equations predict the precise waltz of the planets around the sun, while others determine your insurance rates.

When James Maxwell altered the equations of electricity and magnetism to make them more symmetrical, his new equations showed that light is a wave of electric and magnetic fields, and that light has invisible cousins, including what we now call television and radio waves, radar waves, microwaves, and x-rays.

The contemporary genius Paul Dirac developed an equation to describe an electron. His equation was beautiful, elegant, and clearly right. But the equation also described a particle no one had ever imagined—it resembled a positive electron, but when it combined with an ordinary electron the pair would annihilate into raw energy. Dirac's equation predicted antimatter.

I mention these glories to show that equations can and do have appeal, even poetry. You may need to learn equations that are somewhat less exhalted than Maxwell's or Dirac's. Nevertheless, even the most prosaic equations contain vast amounts of information, and the adage, "a picture is worth a thousand words," can apply to equations as well.

TELESCOPING EQUATIONS

The telescopic technique can help you to assimilate equations of all kinds quickly and with economy of effort.

The process of telescoping equations begins by choosing an easily visualized outline or *skeleton*, decorated with *black boxes* that contain the detailed features. As an example, consider an equation for d, the distance between two points (x, y, z) and (x_o, y_o, z_o):

$$d = [(x-x_o)^2 + (y-y_o)^2 + (z-z_o)^2]^{1/2} \qquad (1)$$

A skeleton or outline of this equation might be seen as

$$d = [\bigcirc]^{1/2} \qquad (2)$$

and the three squared terms can be characterized by ovals (the black boxes):

$$d = [\bigcirc + \bigcirc + \bigcirc]^{1/2} \qquad (3)$$

Finally, the features of the black boxes are filled in. In cases of highly complex equations you can treat the black boxes themselves with the telescopic technique. The black boxes of the present example have the basic form

$$\bigcirc = (x - x_o)^2 \qquad (4)$$

where x can be replaced by y or z. This exploits the symmetry of the three black-box terms. Usually, mere letters serve as black boxes so that s might stand for "sin θ" and K could represent a constant factor like $8\pi/c^3h^2$.

The original equation (1) evolves from the sequence of equations (2), (3), and (4). Of course, it is not necessary to actually sketch the intermediate black boxes; it is enough simply to imagine them. The following sections give examples and exercises.

APPLICATION:
TRIGONOMETRIC IDENTITIES

Use the telescopic approach to learn (or review) the following list of equations. Check your recall of each equation as you go down the list. Then test yourself by covering the most complex side of each equation.

Equation	*Suggested Skeleton*
$\sin^2 x + \cos^2 x = 1$	$s^2 + c^2 = 1$ Here letters serve as black boxes for sine and cosine.
$\sin 2x = 2 \sin x \cos x$	$s2 = 2sc$
$\cos 2x = \cos^2 x - \sin^2 x$	Choose your own.
$\tan 2x = \dfrac{2 \tan x}{1 - \tan^2 x}$	Your choice.
$\cos (x + y) = \cos x \cos y - \sin x \sin y$	$c+ = cc - ss$ The arguments are understood to be ordered: x first, y second.
$\sin (x + y) = \sin x \cos y + \cos x \sin y$	Your choice.
$\tan (x + y) = \dfrac{\tan x + \tan y}{1 - \tan x \tan y}$	Your choice.
$\sin^2 x = \dfrac{1 - \cos 2x}{2}$	Your choice.
$\cos^2 x = \dfrac{1 + \cos 2x}{2}$	Your choice.

APPLICATION:
CALCULUS

The following expressions are standard forms in differential and integral calculus. Apply the telescopic approach to remember the equations, and test yourself by covering the right-hand sides.

Equation	Suggested Skeleton
$$\frac{d}{dx}e^u = e^u\frac{du}{dx}$$	$De = e$ The differential operator is reduced to D, and the factor du/dx is omitted entirely because it occurs in every differentiation.
$$\frac{d}{dx}\ln u = \frac{1}{u}\frac{du}{dx}$$	$D\ln = 1/u$
$$\frac{d}{dx}\sin u = \cos u\frac{du}{dx}$$	Your choice.
$$\frac{d}{dx}\cos u = -\sin u\frac{du}{dx}$$	Your choice.
$$\frac{d}{dx}\sin^{-1} u = \frac{1}{\sqrt{1-u^2}}\frac{du}{dx}$$	$Ds^{-1} = 1/\sqrt{-}$ All the derivatives of inverse trigonometric functions involve $1 \pm u^2$. Only the sign needs to be specified.
$$\frac{d}{dx}\cos^{-1} u = \frac{-1}{\sqrt{1-u^2}}\frac{du}{dx}$$	Your choice.
$$\frac{d}{dx}\tan^{-1} u = \frac{1}{1+u^2}\frac{du}{dx}$$	Your choice.
$$\frac{d}{dx}\cot^{-1} u = \frac{-1}{1+u^2}\frac{du}{dx}$$	Your choice.
$$\int e^u\, du = e^u$$	$\int e = e$ An obvious reduction, but don't forget to replace the differential du in the original.
$$\int \sin u\, du = -\cos u$$	Your choice.
$$\int \cos u\, du = \sin u$$	Your choice.
$$\int e^{au}\sin bu\, du = \frac{e^{au}(a\sin bu - b\cos bu)}{a^2 + b^2}$$	$\int e\, s = e(s - c)/+$
$$\int e^{au}\cos bu\, du = \frac{e^{au}(a\cos bu + b\sin bu)}{a^2 + b^2}$$	Your choice.

A slightly more demanding example is to remember the Laplacian in cylindrical coordinates (ρ, ϕ, z):

$$\nabla^2 U = \frac{1}{\rho} \frac{\partial}{\partial \rho} \left(\rho \frac{\partial U}{\partial \rho} \right) + \frac{1}{\partial^2} \frac{\partial^2 U}{\partial \phi^2} + \frac{\partial^2 U}{\partial z^2}$$

A useful skeleton for this is

$$\nabla^2 = \frac{1}{\rho} \partial(\rho \partial) + \frac{1}{\rho^2} \partial^2 + \partial^2$$

Here U is understood to stand to the right of each term. Moreover, it is understood that the partial derivative symbols correspond to differentiation with respect to ρ, ϕ, and z, in that order. Reconstruct the original Laplacian from the skeleton equation, and try the same approach in the following exercise.

Exercise

Use a telescopic approach to memorize the Laplacian in spherical coordinates (r, θ, ϕ):

$$\nabla^2 U = \frac{1}{r^2} \frac{\partial}{\partial r} \left(r^2 \frac{\partial U}{\partial r} \right) + \frac{1}{r^2 \sin \theta} \frac{\partial}{\partial \theta} \left(\sin \theta \frac{\partial U}{\partial \theta} \right) + \frac{1}{r^2 \sin^2 \theta} \frac{\partial^2 U}{\partial \phi^2}$$

DERIVING EQUATIONS

People with strong mathematical backgrounds usually depend on a relatively small repertoire of memorized equations. Most of the other equations they use are variations involving sign changes, changed variables, or combinations of simpler equations. Simply put, the experts memorize a few equations and derive the rest. If your mathematical experience is limited, you need to rely more on memory than on derivations. Nevertheless, you should follow the example of the experts to the best of your ability—avoid memorizing equations that you can derive quickly and easily.

If, for example, you are aware that the cosine and sine functions obey the following expressions:

$\cos(-y) = \cos y$ (called an *even function*)

$\sin(-y) = -\sin y$ (called an *odd function*)

then you can immediately derive equations for sin $(x - y)$ and cos $(x - y)$ from the corresponding expressions for sin $(x + y)$ and cos $(x + y)$ just by changing y everywhere it appears into $-y$. Thus

$$\cos (x + y) = \cos x \cos y - \sin x \sin y \quad \text{(memorized)}$$

becomes

$$\cos (x - y) = \cos x \cos (-y) - \sin x \sin (-y)$$
$$= \cos x \cos y + \sin x \sin y \quad \text{(derived)}$$

Exercise

Given that

$$\sin (x + y) = \sin x \cos y + \cos x \cos y,$$

show that

$$\sin (x - y) = \sin x \cos y - \cos x \sin y,$$

and

$$\sin 2x = 2 \sin x \cos x.$$

Notice that the first equation is the only one that needs to be memorized—the others are included in it.

READING EQUATIONS BY INTERVIEWING

A scientist or engineer may look at an equation and declare that it is "wrong" or "very interesting." Many people find it remarkable that anyone can "read" an abstract equation and find meaning in it. Happily, even a mathematical novice can get a quick reading of an algebraic expression with just a few considerations.

A simple example can illustrate the point. A tank of helium gas has pressure P and volume V at temperature T (Kelvin). These quantities are related by the equation

$$PV = 8T$$

Suppose, for instance, that for fixed volume the temperature is increased; does the pressure increase or decrease? The simplest way to see this is to fix V at an arbitrary value, say 1, so the equation becomes

$$P = 8T$$

Then give T two successive values, say 1 and 2, and you see that P increases as T increases. Suppose further that the temperature is unchanged but the tank is crushed to a smaller volume. Does pressure increase or decrease? This time, fix T at a value equal to 1 in the original equation, and specify $V = 2$ and $V = 1$ successively. It follows that P increases as V decreases. The equation tells us that pressure increases when the tank is either heated or compressed.

We "interviewed" the equation by posing questions about how one quantity changes as another is increased or decreased. In doing this we gain a familiarity with the equation. Notice that in each case all but two quantities must be held fixed. Then we can see how a change in one quantity affects the other.

Exercise

A planet of mass M has a moon (or an artificial satellite) in circular orbit at a distance d from its center. The time it takes to make one complete revolution is called its *period* and is denoted by t. The relation between M, d, and t is

$$t^2 = k \, \frac{d^3}{M}$$

where k is a (known) constant. Apply the interview approach described in this section to see the effect on the period of changes in orbital distance or planetary mass.

Naturally, there are more sophisticated and penetrating ways to read equations. The topic of curve sketching, treated in analytic geometry and calculus courses, is an extension of our very rudimentary approach.

9
BETTER LEARNING

Using the
techniques for best results

In a few short chapters you've performed electrifying feats of learning and remembering. The techniques you now know are fundamental for the central techniques we have yet to treat. This is an appropriate place to consolidate and briefly discuss how to use techniques most advantageously.

FUNDAMENTALS

When I say that learning techniques should use principles of organization, visualization, and association, it seems as pedestrian as advice to carry an umbrella in threatening weather—sensible though obvious. But modern research indicates that these principles are fundamental, even essential, to learning.

The techniques you've been using are the vehicles of organization, visualization, and association. The telescopic approach is our principal technique for organizing information. It represents the hierarchical kind of thinking used by experts in diverse fields. Substitute imaging is our primary instrument of visualization, and memory chaining is the agent of association. Actually, visualization and association are not neatly separable, and imaging and chaining combine both.

There are several more central techniques to treat, but they are variations and combinations of the three you already know: telescoping, substitute imaging, and memory chaining.

TECHNIQUE VS. FRONTAL ATTACK

Techniques push you to approach material indirectly; the focus is more on how-to-do-it and less on the result. For example, in learning a detailed map good technique demands that you first concentrate on the outline instead of wallowing directly in the particulars. The details come later. Similarly, a pronounced difference between expert problem solvers and novices is that the experts concentrate on the solution ritual while novices stab directly for the answer.

The habit of making a frontal attack on material is the greatest hindrance to good technique. It is natural to mount a direct assault, but battles conducted without strategy and tactics are wasteful even when they succeed. When you apply techniques, focus on the procedures, and the results will follow.

No doubt people have many reasons to resist indirect approaches to learning. Some are concerned that techniques are games and not "true" learning. This is really an argument in favor of techniques, because game playing is a natural way of learning that is programmed into the genes of intelligent animals. A deeper, but unspoken notion is that learning must be painful to be effective—a sad commentary on our educational experiences.

Perhaps the most mistaken concern is that the time spent in applying procedures is time away from learning. Be assured that you are learning as you apply techniques. This is true even if you don't succeed in completing the procedure. Your concentration and exposure to the material are greatest when you use techniques. Take the time to apply learning techniques—your time will not be wasted.

REAL LIFE

Alas, learning techniques are not a panacea. Techniques make learning easier and more effective, but not automatic.

"Real life" applications don't always follow clear blueprints. Sometimes you will encounter material that is fuzzier or more tortured than any presented in this book. Do not panic. Remember that you can always resort to your old methods, but you probably won't need to. As your experience grows, you can be more flexible and adapt the techniques to unusual cases.

Techniques do not replace good sense. It takes alertness—a "mental set"—to be ready to apply techniques. Simple, routine exchanges of information rarely warrant such intense concentration (except for practice). Life can become clumsy indeed for people trying to use techniques indiscriminately.

ON STUDY

Review and rest are important factors in effective study. Here are some guidelines to get the best results from review and rest.

Learning techniques reveal that the human memory is much stronger than people imagine. It is a curious paradox that memory is also less reliable and less accurate than the public believes. We fill gaps in our knowledge with imagination, so that the facts become distorted. Worse, we suffer from a flood of forgetting after study; an 80 percent loss of recall can occur in twenty-four hours. You've noticed that your memory is much more persistent when you use techniques, but some loss is inevitable.

Frequent reviews halt these memory distortions and decay. A good program of review is to rehearse the material at intervals of five to ten minutes, one day, one week, one month, and six months after the initial learning. Learning is then virtually permanent. The review sessions should take only a few minutes for each day of initial learning.

Study is also more effective with frequent rest breaks of five to ten minutes. Two factors help to make breaks useful: (1) We tend to remember best the first and last items in a study sequence, and breaks introduce more "first" and "last" items. (2) We remember more about five to ten minutes after studying than we do immediately after. A rest allows this consolidation to take place.

The optimum duration of a study period depends in part on the material. The longest periods should be given to conceptual material and the shortest to routine memory tasks. Most study periods should be under an hour and over fifteen minutes before resting. Then you can consolidate with a few moments of review before continuing to the next study period.

10
MAPPING THOUGHTS

A central technique
for summarizing facts and ideas

The name of your first love or a mention of your home town can stir a storm of memories. Other words, phrases, and images remind you of facts and ideas. It is not surprising that such key words play an important role in recalling readings, lectures, and films, particularly when combined with other techniques. These applications are treated in later chapters. This chapter shows how to choose key words and arrange them in maps—thought-maps that enable you to retrieve ideas and facts.

CHOOSING KEY WORDS OR IMAGES

It takes attention and effort to summarize a thought with key words. In fact, your efforts at choosing key words are an important part of the learning process.

For example, the following sentence is taken from an article about the history of Chief Justice Burger's court:

> Warren E. Burger's tenure as Chief Justice of the Supreme Court is characterized by decisions that are narrowly constructed technical compromises that avoid sweeping legal principles.

You want to select key words—the fewer, the better—that will remind you of the central idea. Certainly this process is subjective, and there are many possible choices. I prefer the key word *narrow* to remind me that technical compromises are characteristic of the Burger court. Other choices are *sweeping legal principles* or (better) *sweeping;* these work even though they suggest the opposite of the "narrow" idea. You can easily remember that the original idea is the antithesis of your key word. *Burger* or *Supreme Court* are poor choices in this context because these are the subjects of an entire article and therefore not sufficiently specific to unlock the "narrow" idea.

Key images are often preferable to key words. For the previous example, an image of a narrow hamburger is a vivid reminder of narrow legal decisions by the Burger court. It is convenient to understand that the term *key word* includes key images as well.

Exercise

As you can see in the chapter on reading, only rarely do you need to remember ideas sentence by sentence. As an exercise, however, it is worthwhile to write key words for each of the six sentences in the abstract below. Choose key words that will remind you of the basic idea or fact in each sentence.

Abstract: Components of Memory

(1) Recent research in human memory suggests that memory functions can be separated into three components. (2) The first is sensory memory, with which we momentarily grasp sights and sounds all around us. (3) These sensory impressions last less than one second before they fade away. (4) The second component of memory, short-term memory, is associated with consciousness; it holds the thought-of-the-moment. (5) Finally, long-term memory is the component that stores huge amounts of information more or less permanently. (6) We become conscious of sensory memories and stored long-term memories only when they are moved into short-term memory, where they can be held under continual attention.

Use your list of key words to see how much you can remember about each of the original statements. Of course, you do not need to repeat the original statement verbatim. Most likely you will require one review to secure all the statements in this dense paragraph.

Key words are more effective when they are arranged in maps. Maps are constructed with a telescopic approach, whereby you first find a central idea (the *core point*) and then decorate it with key words for subordinate ideas and facts.

The paragraph of the last exercise can serve as an example. Perhaps the most central statement is that there are three components to memory; a natural key word is *three*. The names of these components can be seen as subordinate to this. We sketch this situation in the form of a map.

Adding further details introduces the functions and features of the components:

These maps of key words are *thought maps* (some authors use the term *mind map*). Notice how easily you can remember the abstract in thought-map form as compared with the linear sequence of key words you used in the last exercise.

You may have noticed that my thought map does not contain all the information it might. For instance, the information in sentence (6), indicating that we can be aware of a memory only if it is moved into short term, is not represented explicitly. The reason is that I expect to remember the idea simply by seeing the key word *conscious* in context.

Most written material is filled with small details that support the central points and add color and clarity to the message. Usually it is quite unimportant to remember such minutiae. Using a telescopic approach, you can construct a thought map to include a little or a lot of detail. We can say that our thought-map example includes details to the "second level," although this terminology is rather loose, since some items might be treated in more layers of detail than others.

FINDING CORE POINTS

A thought map is like a box full of related ideas and facts. There is one central point, the core point, that is used as a label and summarizes the contents of the box. The most effective way to boost reading comprehension is to find these core points.

The search is easier when you recognize that the core point is the most *general* idea in a thought map. It summarizes the broad idea, but not the details, of the map. In fact, the core point is not always the most informative point in the map. Rather, it is the most encompassing label for the box of ideas; it is the umbrella statement that covers the other statements in the thought map.

The main distinction you must make is between *general* and *specific* (or detailed) statements. In the following "paragraphs" the sentences are out of order. In each one, find the most general idea in the group. Check that each of the other sentences either elaborates, explains, or gives details about the sentence you choose.

Exercise

Choose the most general statement from the following scrambled paragraphs. Answers are given below.

Paragraph 1
A. Shade trees around the home cut down on light for indoor plants.
B. The direction which a window faces determines the quality of light coming through it.
C. Plant growth depends on how much natural light is available.
D. A house next door can also block light.

A. Certainly, the call to "come here" should be obeyed.

B. A dog's welfare depends on its having been taught some basic discipline.

C. Training your pet to walk on a leash is important.

D. It does not break the spirit of a dog to obey voice commands.

Paragraph 3

A. A look into the near future will provide you with tasks to accomplish.

B. Make a priority list of those tasks to be accomplished today.

C. A few basic steps can help you to manage your time.

D. Allocate hours or minutes to each task on the list.

E. Then put the day's schedule on your calendar and follow it.

Answers

Paragraph 1

A. Shade trees are specific agents that reduce the light.

B. Window direction is a specific factor affecting the quality of light.

C. This is the most general statement. All others are specifics regarding "how much natural light is available."

D. A house next door is a specific agent that reduces light.

Paragraph 2

A. Obeying the call to "come here" is a specific part of dog discipline.

B. This is the most general statement. All others mention specific disciplines.

C. Walking on a leash is a specific discipline.

D. This sentence is easily mistaken as the most general, but when you compare this with sentence B, you see that voice commands are part of basic discipline.

Paragraph 3

A. This sentence is often mistaken as the most general. Comparison with sentence C, however, shows that collecting tasks is just a specific step in managing your time.

B. Making a priority list is a specific step in managing your time.

C. This is the most general statement.
D. Allocating time to tasks is a specific step in managing your time.
E. Making a schedule is another specific step in managing your time.

As you look for core points, it helps to know that the central idea in a paragraph is in either the first or last sentence in about 80 percent of cases. As a consequence, a core point is most likely to come from these sentences. (The term *topic sentence* is avoided here because core points are more general—core points can extend beyond a single paragraph, and topic sentences cannot.)

Where are the central ideas of the other 20% of all paragraphs? They may be anywhere in the paragraph. In some cases the central idea is not stated, and you are left to infer your own.

MAP STRUCTURE

It is useful to practice to sketch thought maps for a few paragraphs. Ovals are used to represent core points, and circles represent supporting points. As an example, examine the map we construct for the following paragraph:

(1) A few basic steps can help you to manage your time. (2) First, a look into the near future will provide you with tasks to accomplish. (3) Next, make a priority list of those tasks to be accomplished today. (4) Allocate hours or minutes to each task on the list. (5) Then put the day's schedule on your calendar and follow it.

The corresponding thought map is shown in Figure 10.1. Notice that it shows the direct relation between points (3) and (4).

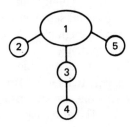

FIGURE 10.1.

Exercises

1. Find the core point in the paragraph below using the criteria of (1) generality and (2) sentence placement. Sketch a thought map using sentence numbers as labels.

> (1) Male body builders use exercise and diet to develop special qualities. (2) Huge muscle size or "bulk" is the most obvious attribute. (3) But equally important is the sharp definition of the muscles that makes them stand out like steel cables under the skin. (4) Good definition requires fat-free musculature to reveal the fine lines. (5) More subtle, but perhaps most coveted, is symmetry, where the body has a graceful, balanced shape.

Now key words, core points, and mapping can be put together again. See Figure 10.2 for one possibility for the thought map of the time-management example.

FIGURE 10.2.

2. Sketch a thought map of the body-building paragraph with key words rather than numbers. (Your number-map should look like the number-map for the time-management example.)

So far we used thought maps for single paragraphs. This is too limiting. Thought maps embrace ideas and facts that transcend paragraphs and sentences. Often you can use just one map for a section of many paragraphs. Occasionally you may want to map a single informative sentence.

It is acceptable, even desirable, to create thought maps with some imaginative forms. However, try to make them easy to visualize. A few variations are shown in Figure 10.3.

Thought maps are instruments of telescopic and visual thinking.

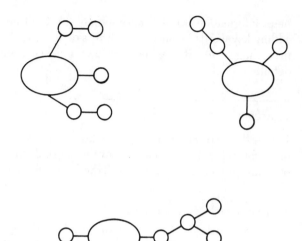

FIGURE 10.3.

They are the basis for reading and note-taking techniques described in later chapters. And maps are graphics of mental organization—like words, you can think with them without writing them down.

SUMMARY

Choosing Key Words and Images: Choose key words or key images that seem best to remind you of an idea or fact. The fewer key words for each idea, the better. Feel free to choose key words or images that express the antithesis of an idea—you will recognize it as such.

Finding Core Points: A core point is the most *general idea in a thought map; other points in the map are specifics* relating to the core. Look for general encompassing core points.

Core points can often be found among the first or last sentences of paragraphs.

Constructing Thought Maps: (1) Write key words or images for the core point of the map; (2) Attach key words for a first level of subordinate information to the core point; (3) Continue the process of adding key words for successive layers of detail to the key words of the preceding level. Stop when you have reached a satisfactory level of detail.

Exercise

Follow the steps in the summary to devise a single thought map for each of the following short articles. Draw the map only to about a second level of detail, and see that you can recall the basic information from the map.

Remove Scratch Marks on Glass

Are scratches detracting from your windows, sliding glass doors, or watch face? You can repair these and other glass scratches simply with household products.

An ordinary cleansing powder like Bon Ami can be used as a buffing powder. Of course, you can buy commercial buffing powders from many paint and glass stores.

The powder should be applied with a damp cloth or towel and rubbed well. A precaution: tempered glass may shatter from the heat of machine buffing. We recommend hand buffing for this reason.

Scratches may be too deep for buffing if you can feel them with your fingernail. You may still remove the scratches with much rubbing, but a wavy effect can develop. Of course, this may be preferable to scratches.

Touch, Taste and the Desire to Eat*

How important is cool creaminess to the appeal of ice cream, juicy chewiness to the allure of a steak, or crunchiness to the craving for an apple? Studies of pigeons and rats have recently shown that the feel of food in the mouth is a more important factor in the desire to eat than taste is.

Traditionally, we think of taste as the most significant oral element in eating. But Dr. H. Philip Zeigler, an animal-behavior researcher from New York's Hunter College, decided to investigate how the *feel* of food is related to appetite.

To do this, he severed the nerves that provide tactile sensation in pigeons and rats, leaving alone their ability to taste. Zeigler observed that in both

*This material originally appeared in *Science Digest*, April 1981. Reprinted by permission of Mitchel L. Zoler.

species this caused a sudden and dramatic drop in the amount of time spent eating. Since the animals were still able to eat, Zeigler concluded that they did not want to eat—their appetites simply died.

A striking aspect of Zeigler's discovery was that the loss of interest in eating occurred immediately after the mouth's tactile nerves were severed. The animals did not have to eat first for loss of appetite to take place.

During several weeks of abstaining almost entirely from food, the weights of the pigeons and rats fell by over 20 percent. Eventually many of them resumed their normal feeding patterns, but they never ate in sufficient quantity to regain normal adult weight.

In a separate experiment using another test group, Zeigler severed the nerves that transmit *taste* perception to the brain. In contrast, he found the loss of feeding activity to be minimal and transient. His conclusion: The inability to feel food diminishes, specifically and dramatically, the desire to eat, whereas the inability to taste food does not.

The imagination jumps to the notion that this could lead to a remedy that millions of overeaters are seeking. Zeigler, however, dismisses the feasibility of severing nerves in people—the complexity of nerve structures would offer too many opportunities for surgical disaster. He does speculate, though, that elimination of oral touch sensation, and hence appetite, may be possible by altering the action of certain nerve-signal chemicals. Development of this form of treatment has not even been attempted, and Zeigler speculates it would take at least 10 years of intensive research.

Development of Language and Speech*

Normal children have, at birth, the potential to walk and to talk, although as babies they can do neither. They are genetically endowed with the appropriate neurophysical systems, but time is needed for these systems to develop and mature. The brain is approximately 40% the size it will attain by adulthood; the more peripheral areas, the vocal tract and the legs, await the anatomical change and the development of motor-sensory associations appropriate to talking and walking. At 6 months, children sit up and *babble* in meaningless vocal play. By the arrival of the first birthday, they may have started to walk and to name things. By the second birthday, they may be putting two words together for rudimentary telegraphic sentences, and by the fourth, they will have mastered the essential rules of the language of their elders. The rapidity and apparent ease with which children learn language is a phenomenon of childhood and can

*From *Speech Science Primer* by Gloria J. Borden and Katherine S. Harris. Copyright © 1980, the Williams & Wilkins Co., Baltimore. Courtesy the Williams & Wilkins Company and Gloria J. Borden, Ph.D., Speech & Hearing Ctr., Temple Univ., Coll. of Liberal Arts, Philadelphia 19140.

never be repeated with such ease by adults. Many adults learn new languages, especially those who already know several languages, but the time most conducive to learning languages is before puberty. Wilder Penfield, the Canadian neurophysiologist, put the cut-off age at about 15. The best time for learning language, however, is during the first 4 years.

What children universally accomplish with spontaneity and speed, psychologists, linguists, and speech scientists have laboriously analyzed with only moderate success. The question they ask is: how do children acquire language? Theorists on this subject can be generally divided into two groups. One group of theorists analyzes language development in terms of learning principles. The other group analyzes language development in terms of an innate propensity for language. Perhaps the most currently popular view is that only the details or individual items of a particular language are learned, while the structural and creative underpinnings universal to all languages are inherited.

Character and Characterization*

Character is the primary material from which plots are created, for incidents are developed through the speech and behavior of dramatic personages. Characterization is the playwright's means of differentiating one personage from another.

The first level of characterization is *physical* and concerns such basic facts as sex, age, size, and color. Sometimes a dramatist does not supply all of this information, but it is present whenever the play is produced, since actors necessarily give concrete form to the characters.

The second level is *social*. It includes a character's economic status, profession or trade, religion, family relationships—all those factors that place him in his environment.

The third level is *psychological*. It reveals a character's habitual responses, desires, motivations, likes and dislikes—the inner workings of the mind. Since drama most often arises from conflicting desires, the psychological is the most essential level of characterization.

The fourth level is *moral*. It is most often used in serious plays, especially tragedies. Moral decisions differentiate characters more fully than any other type, since such decisions cause a character to examine his own motives, in the process of which his true nature is revealed both to himself and to the audience.

A playwright can emphasize one or more of these levels and may assign

*From *The Essential Theatre* by Oscar G. Brockett. Copyright © 1980, 1976 by Holt, Rinehart and Winston. Reprinted by permission of Holt, Rinehart and Winston, CBS College Publishing.

many or few traits, depending on *how the character functions in the play*. For example, the audience needs to know very little about a maid who appears only to announce dinner. The principal characters, on the other hand, should be drawn in considerable depth.

A character is revealed in several ways: through *descriptions in stage directions, prefaces, or other explanatory material* not part of the dialogue; through *what the character says;* through *what others say about him;* and, most important, through *what he does*.

Dramatic characters are usually both *typified* and *individualized*. If a character were totally unlike any person the spectators had ever known, they would be unable to understand him. But the audience may be dissatisfied unless the playwright goes beyond this typification and gives his characters individualizing traits. The best dramatic characters are usually easily recognizable types with some unusual or complex qualities.

A playwright may be concerned with making his characters *sympathetic* or *unsympathetic*. Normally, sympathetic characters are given major virtues and lesser foibles, while the reverse is true of unsympathetic characters. The more a character is made either completely good or bad, the more he is apt to be unacceptable as a truthful reflection of human behavior. Acceptability varies with the type of play. Melodrama, for example, oversimplifies human psychology and clearly divides characters into good or evil. Tragedy, on the other hand normally depicts more complex forces at work both within and without characters and requires greater depth of characterization.

11
READING

Techniques for improving
reading speed, comprehension, and recall

Jane S., a prominent state official, prepares for news conferences by reading reports with agonizing intensity. Her desk is littered with coffee cups and cigarette butts as her eyes burn down each page—line by line, fact after fact. She is reading to remember.

Jane's approach is painfully familiar to most of us. When the information is important, we fear that reading less carefully will cause us to miss important points. We are sure we will remember less with a faster, less intense reading. Fortunately, these concerns are misguided—there is a better way.

Not every reading needs to be remembered in detail. Usually, it is sufficient to remember only the broadest topic outlines. Of course, you need to remember details when you are being tested, when you present the material to others, or when the particulars are important for the routine conduct of your business or profession. In other cases it makes more sense simply to skim and file the information with no attempt to remember it.

You recognize these extreme goals in reading: reading to re-member and reading for a general idea. We would like to remember everything we read, but the reality is that we must invest time and effort to increase both original learning and recall. It is more efficient to use high-speed techniques of previewing and skimming for general content, and a telescopic approach for graphic recall.

THE FORMAT OF BOOKS, REPORTS, AND ARTICLES

The time you spend in organizing reading material is not wasted. Indeed, organizing can be the most useful step in the learning process, especially for complex or dense material. The first step in this organization is to be clearly aware of the format of books, reports, and articles.

Textbooks generally have a format of chapters, sections, and paragraphs (see Figure 11.1). Of course, there are variations on this theme. Often the chapters are themselves organized into broader subject headings; a physics test may include the headings "Mechanics," "Heat," "Waves," and so on, each of which comprise several chapters. Another variation has sections subdivided into subsections; an art text may have a section entitled "The Renaissance Period" that is further divided into the subsections "Early Renaissance" and "Late Renaissance."

Long reports generally have formats similar to books, but a good report often has the additional virtue of having a succinct abstract and a conclusion or summary. Take advantage of these attributes and read the abstract and the conclusion or summary first.

Articles and short reports usually have a format similar to a single chapter in a textbook. Often, especially in shorter articles, the section captions are omitted, and the copy appears as an unbroken list of paragraphs. In these cases you can gain an advantage by imposing your own section headings.

FIGURE 11.1.

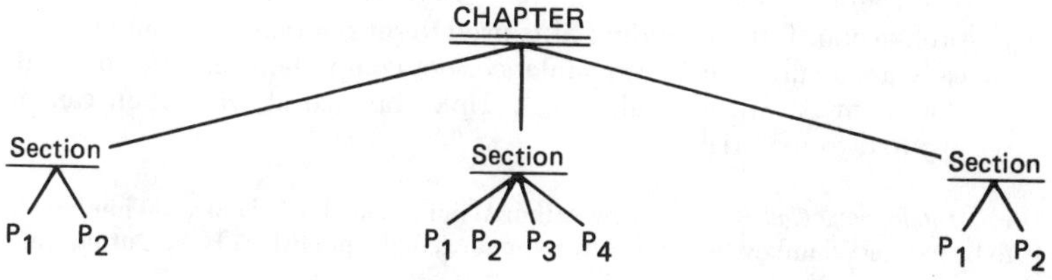

Review the organization of a book or long article before you read it. Examine any table of contents, section headings, and abstract or summary to get some idea of where the text is going and how it will get there.

READING FOR A GENERAL IDEA

The fastest reading techniques exploit the fact that you can catch the overall meaning in readings without reading every word. This is a reasonable approach to avoiding unnecessary reading. Many people claim reading rates well above 1000 words per minute, although the physiological limit seems to be less than 800 words per minute. These readers are not lying—they are reading well without actually seeing all the words.

People expect too much from rapid-reading techniques because of publicity about speed reading. Some limitations of speed reading are described by Arthur and Linda Whimbey in their book *Intelligence Can Be Taught:**

> Speed reading instructs the student to skim down the center of the page, rather than reading from left to right, and to aim for a rate of 1000 or more words per minute. In this way, no sentence is completely skipped, but each is merely touched on. Theoretically, speed reading (when pursued by a person who is already a good reader) differs from poor reading in that it does emphasize attention to comprehension and active construction of meaning; there is a mental set to try to understand. But the question is, How much can possibly be gathered and understood while the reader's eyes are racing directly down the center of a page?
>
> It should be obvious from the previous discussion of reading as thinking and analysis of relations, that speed reading cannot possibly impart comprehension of new and complex ideas, but can only provide a superficial acquaintance with topics. For many purposes, and much reading material, this may be all that is required. But more cannot be expected.
>
> The claim is sometimes made that speed reading will triple your comprehension. But the reading tests used to substantiate this claim statistically are really tests of acquaintance, not comprehension. The only fair statement is: Speed reading will triple the rate at which you can be exposed to material.

*From *Intelligence Can Be Taught* by Arthur Whimbey with Linda Shaw Whimbey. © 1975 by Arthur Whimbey. Reprinted by permission of the publisher, E. P. Dutton, Inc.

The reading rates of University of Michigan professors who were tested averaged about 300 words per minute. These are highly intelligent professionals with lifelong practice in taking ideas and information from the printed page—but 300 words per minute is seen as deficient according to speed-reading advocates. More likely, the deficiency lies in how success in reading is being assessed. Arthur Whimbey makes it clear:

> A speed reading class I attended had as its stated objective: "increasing reading rate while not dropping below 70 percent comprehension." One student, for example, started at 400 words a minute at 90 percent comprehension and "progressed" to 1300 words a minute at 70 percent comprehension. The instructor of the course argued that 70 percent of 1300 (which equals 910) was more than 90 percent of 400 (equals 360) so that comprehension per time unit was increased. The weakness in this statistical juggling is evident. In an absolute sense, 70 percent is lower comprehension than 90 percent; 70 percent comprehension means that 30 percent of the material is missed. I personally do not want a surgeon who understands 70 percent of his medical text, or an automobile mechanic with only 70 percent comprehension of auto repair. For that matter, when I read a joke in the course of a novel, I don't care to come away with only 70 percent of the punch line.*

You can get a general idea of long and difficult readings by *previewing:* read the first two paragraphs, then read only the first sentence of the following paragraphs, and read the last two paragraphs. Also read all topic and section headings.

Previewing is suitable for a quick overview of heavy, long readings like textbook chapters, and for long articles and reports. It can increase your reading rate five- or ten-fold, with as much as 50 percent comprehension. You can always decide whether you want a closer reading.

Articles usually orient the reader within the first two paragraphs and summarize in the last two. Most importantly, a majority of core points are given in the first sentences of paragraphs. These sentences, together with topic and section headings, reveal much of the basic content.

Another technique for rapid reading is *skimming.* It is slower but more thorough than previewing. And, of course, it is faster than standard reading. Authorities in rapid reading usually refer to skimming as

*Ibid.

picking out only a few key words from every line. Skimming is used here as a search—a search for core points.

You found core points for thought maps by looking for general, inclusive points—usually from among the beginnings or ends of paragraphs. Skimming, for our purposes, is making this search while only glancing at the subordinate facts, details, supporting statements, and specifics of all kinds.

Skimming focuses on central points, but peripheral information rubs off in the search. This technique is valuable, not only for general ideas, but as a preliminary step in reading-to-remember.

READING IN HIGH GEAR

Standard reading is what most of us do when there is no need to rush or memorize. Previewing and skimming have uses, as does the heavy artillery of reading-to-remember, but these should be reserved for when they are needed. Contrary to the opinion of some advocates of speed reading, there is no shame in just reading.

Perhaps you want to continue "just reading" but in a higher gear. You can improve comprehension and increase speed by *clustering*—reading words in groups.

To cluster, read in groups of two, three, or four words at a glance. Here is a sentence as you might cluster it:

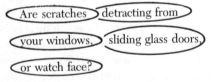

You can cluster right away, but it may take several days of practice before it becomes comfortable. Do not rush at first. Concentrate on reading in lumps, and gradually press for more speed over a week or two.

READING TO REMEMBER

Reading and remembering difficult material is always hard study, but it can be made much easier with a telescopic approach. The basic idea is to see the structure of the reading in layers: the overall format, core points, first level of specifics, and so on. And usually each layer is treated in a separate pass through the material. The information is recorded in thought maps, which are easily memorized.

In most of what follows I will have you focus on reading and mapping for higher levels of detail—as if you were preparing for a test or presentation. It will then be easy to relax your approach for less demanding cases.

The first "reading" should be a mere skim of a section. Try to answer only one question: in the broadest terms, what are the most central ideas or facts in this section? Some sections may encompass only one fundamental idea, others may include several. Surprisingly, sections often contain no truly basic points. This is frequently true of introductory sections that orient the reader to the topic.

The central points are usually easy to find in clearly written material, but texts and reports can be notoriously opaque. The burden then falls to you to select core points, and often there are several alternative choices, some giving better organization than others. In such cases, it is worth taking a few moments to decide on a set of core points that appear to best reflect the structure of the information.

When you have found the central points (if any) in a section, write key words or images for each. These will serve as the cores of thought maps.

Now reread the section just closely enough to identify a first level of detail, and include key words for these details on the thought maps. Continue rereading and adding to the maps until you attain the desired level of detail. Bear in mind that you do not need to include every nuance on the thought map. Your natural memory will fish up associated points pertaining to the recorded key words and images. When you finish the first section, repeat the process for succeeding sections.

You want to be flexible with this procedure. Often, subordinate points are so clearly bristling from a core point that it would be silly to wait for a later pass to include them. In other cases, only an occasional detail needs to be attached to a point to avoid another reading. But whenever things are difficult or cloudy, it helps to leave specifics for another pass.

The result of the full procedure is a set of notes—thought maps. These are easily memorized as they were recorded, in a layered sequence. The cores of thought maps are linked in a memory chain, then a first level of specifics is associated with each core, etc. For the present, it will be enough to record the maps. The chapter on notes will give a more detailed treatment of memorizing thought maps.

Does it take more time to execute repeated readings instead of reading very closely just once? No, not for equivalent results. There are clear benefits of organization and internal association in using this iterative technique (as with all telescopic approaches). Moreover, the readings are rapid because the reader focuses on one level at a time with a minimum of regression, a major cause of slow reading.

DOING LESS

Reading-to-remember is a powerful but demanding collection of techniques. I recommend that you first become comfortable with the full procedure, although you can usually have excellent reading recall with much less effort.

You may, for example, read for the central points only (the cores of the maps). As you read, you can link these points without writing any notes. An occasional important detail can be linked mentally with the core points. Even this simplified version of the full approach greatly improves a reader's ability to remember. I find that I use this lean approach for most of my reading-to-remember.

Many readers underline or highlight readings. These approaches may be regarded as substitutes for sketching thought maps. If highlighting is your preference, try not to highlight too much; students' textbooks are sometimes 70 percent or more highlighted—a sure waste of effort. Highlight only material that you would otherwise summarize on a thought map. Several people have reported that highlighting in two colors, one for core points and one for details, helped their reading recall.

SUMMARY

Reading for a General Idea: Previewing is used for long difficult readings. Read the first two paragraphs, the first sentence of the following paragraphs, and the last two paragraphs. Include all topic and section headings.

Skimming is searching for core points while only glancing at the subordinate points. Look especially for general, inclusive points from the beginnings or ends of paragraphs.

Reading in High Gear: Clustering gives more speed and comprehension to standard reading. Read in clusters of two to four words at a glance.

Reading to Remember: This is a telescopic approach where the structure of the reading is seen in layers: format, core points, first level specifics, etc. The information is recorded in thought maps.

Examine the formats of books, reports, and articles before reading. Look at any table of contents and at chapter and section headings. Read any abstract, conclusions, or summary first. Try to see where the text is going and how it will get there.

Reading and Mapping: (1) Skim a section (or the equivalent) to find the central point(s). Record key words for each central point; these serve as cores for maps. (2) Repeatedly reread the section, adding a level of details to the thought maps with each reading. Stop when you have treated enough detail. Do not try to record every particular—the maps will remind you of more detail than you have recorded. (3) Repeat the second step for each section.

For most purposes, excellent reading recall is obtained with far fewer steps than the full procedure outlined above. For example, the second step may be eliminated entirely when fine details are unimportant.

Exercise

Apply the Summary's reading and mapping instructions to the reading selections that follow. Construct thought maps to a second level of details (where warranted), and check that you can reconstruct the basic information in each article from the maps. (Save these thought maps. The chapter on notes shows how to memorize them.)

Plot*

Plot is often considered merely the summary of a play's incidents, but—though it includes the story line—it also refers to the organization of all the elements into a meaningful pattern. Plot is thus the over-all structure of a play.

The Beginning. The beginning of a play usually establishes the place, the occasion, the characters, the mood, the theme, and the type of probability. A play is somewhat like coming upon previously unknown places and persons. Initially, the novelty may excite interest, but, as the facts about the place and people are established, interest either wanes or increases. The playwright is faced with a double problem: he must give essential information but at the same time make the audience want to stay and see more.

The beginning of a play thus involves *exposition,* or the setting forth of information—about earlier events, the identity of the characters, and the present situation. While exposition is an unavoidable part of the opening scenes, it is not confined to them, for in most plays background information is only gradually revealed.

The amount of exposition required is partly determined by the *point of attack,* the moment at which the story is taken up. Shakespeare uses an early point of attack (that is, he begins the play near the beginning of the story and tells it chronologically). Thus he needs little exposition. Greek tragic dramatists, on the other hand, use later points, which require that many previous events be summarized for the audience's benefit. They thus actually show only the final parts of their stories.

Playwrights motivate giving exposition in many ways. For example, Ibsen most frequently introduces a character who has returned after a long absence. Answers to his questions about happenings while he was away supply the needed background information. On the other hand, in a nonrealistic play essential exposition may be given in a monologue. Many of Euripides' tragedies, for example, open with a monologue-prologue summarizing past events. In a musical play, exposition may be given in song and dance.

In most plays from the past, attention is usually focused early on a question, potential conflict, or theme. The beginning of such plays therefore includes what may be called an *inciting incident,* an occurrence that sets the main action in motion. In Sophocles' *Oedipus the King* a plague is destroying the city of Thebes; Oedipus has sought guidance from the oracle at Delphi, who declares that the murderer of King Laius must be found and punished before the plague can end. This is the event (introduced in the prologue) that sets the action in motion.

The inciting incident usually leads directly to a *major dramatic question* around which the play is organized, although this question may change as the play progresses. For example, the question first raised in *Oedipus the King* is: Will the murderer of Laius be found and the city saved? Later this question changes as interest shifts to the question of Oedipus' guilt.

Not all plays, especially recent ones, include inciting incidents or clearly identifiable major dramatic questions. All have focal points, nevertheless, frequently a theme or controlling idea around which the action is centered.

The Middle. The middle of a play is normally composed of a series of complications. A *complication* is any new element which changes the direction of the action—the discovery of new information, for example, or the arrival of a character. The substance of most complications is *discovery* (any occurrence of sufficient importance to alter the direction of action). Discoveries may involve objects (a wife discovers in her husband's pocket a weapon of the kind used in a murder), persons (a young man discovers that his rival in love is his brother), facts (a young man about to leave home discovers that his mother has cancer), values (a woman discovers that self-esteem is more important than marriage), or self (a man discovers that he has been acting from purely selfish motives when he thought he was acting out of love for his children). Each complication normally has a beginning, middle, and end—its own development, climax, and resolution—just as does the play as a whole. Usually the complications are overlapping rather than strung together in a series.

Means other than discoveries may be used to precipitate complications. Natural disasters (earthquakes, storms, shipwrecks, automobile accidents) are sometimes used. These are apt to seem especially contrived if they resolve the problem (for example, if the villain were to be killed in an automobile accident and as a result the struggle automatically ended).

The series of complications culminates in the *crisis*, or turning point of the action. For example, in *Oedipus the King* Oedipus sets out to discover the murderer of Laius; the crisis comes when Oedipus realizes that he himself is the guilty person. Not all plays have a clear-cut series of complications leading to a crisis. *Waiting for Godot*, for example, is less concerned with a progressing action than with a static condition. Nevertheless, interest is maintained by the frequent introduction of new elements.

The End. The final portion of a play, often called the *resolution* or *dénouement* (unraveling or untying), extends from the crisis to the final curtain. It varies in length. It serves to tie off the various strands of action and to answer the questions raised earlier. It brings the situation back to a state of balance and satisfies audience expectations.

The Black Death*

One third of the people of the world dead, 36% of the universities closed, 50% of the clergy dead. Europe devastated in only three years. Towns

*Adapted from *The Man-Made World,* published by McGraw-Hill, © 1971 by Polytechnic Institute of Brooklyn. All Rights Reserved. Reprint publication is not an endorsement by the original copyright owner.

deserted, farms lying idle, and gloom over the entire continent. This is the picture in 1351 at the end of the Black Death, the bubonic plague that swept from Asia throughout the civilized world in the great epidemic of the fourteenth century.

Bubonic plague is a disease spread primarily by fleas which usually live on rodents. The disease is spread among the rodents (often rats) by the fleas, and humans contract the disease from fleas, especially when the rat population decreases because of disease. The fleas then seek human hosts.

Actually, the bubonic plague of the fourteenth century had three different forms. The first, involving bubons, or boils, at the lymph nodes in the groin or armpits, is spread primarily by fleas. In the second form, in which pneumonia is involved with disease of the lungs, transmission can occur directly between human beings. The third form, involving the nervous system, is highly contagious and causes death within hours.

The first recorded instance of the plague occurred in the Near East in the eleventh century B.C. Apparently, there are regions of northern India and central Asia where the plague is continually latent. Worldwide epidemics have started there at least three times during the last 2000 years.

The first great pandemic (an epidemic covering the civilized world) occurred in the sixth century A.D. Lasting fifty years, "Justinian's plague" involved the Roman world and certainly was one factor in the disintegration of the Roman Empire.

The latest pandemic started in the middle of the last century in China, reached Hong Kong by the start of this century, and then spread throughout the world from the Chinese ports. With an estimated 10 million deaths in India, the epidemic was most serious in Asia. With the concept of quarantine established in Europe by about 1720, the emphasis on sanitation and hospitalization during the last century, and improved urban sewage-disposal and rat-control systems, the epidemic did not seriously affect the western world. In more recent years, particularly with the use of antibiotics, bubonic plague has been well controlled with only 200 deaths per year over the last decade.

The great pandemic of the fourteenth century started in northern India. It is not known why the plague began its spread. Apparently, the rodent population which normally carries the disease was forced to migrate, because of food shortage, excessive rain, earthquakes, or other reasons.

The plague reached western Europe in 1347 and primary effects lasted for the next three years during which more than 30 million Europeans died, or a third of the population. Actually the epidemic followed the normal pattern and recurred over the next two centuries before finally subsiding, but the term "Black Death" usually refers to the first catastrophic three years.

While the plague undoubtedly was brought to Europe in several ways, historians often spotlight the primary source as the Tartar siege of the Crimean port of Kaffa in 1347. As so often happens in war, thousands of men were brought together in unsanitary conditions, in this case in a region infested by rats. The Tartars began dying by the thousands and finally dispersed.

Once the siege was lifted, ships immediately sailed for Genoa, Italy. When the ships reached Genoa, they were sent away and then carried the plague to Sicily, Spain, and northern Africa.

The chronology of the epidemic gives a picture of the plague fanning out from the Italy-Sicily start northward, westward, and eastward:

1348   N. Africa, Spain, France
1349   Austria, Hungary, Switzerland, Netherlands, northern Germany, England
1350   Scandinavia, Scotland, Ireland

The size of the catastrophe is emphasized by the death rates, which varied from ⅛ to ⅔. Investigations of the death toll in Europe at that time are reported by W. Langer:

As reported by chroniclers of the time, the mortality figures were so incredibly high that modern scholars long regarded them with skepticism. Recent detailed and rigorously conducted analyses indicate, however, that many of the reports were substantially correct. It is now generally accepted that at least a quarter of the European population was wiped out in the first epidemic of 1348 through 1350, and that in the next fifty years the total mortality rose to more than a third of the population. The incidence of the disease and the mortality rate varied, of course, from place to place. Florence was reduced in population from 99,000 to 15,000; Hamburg apparently lost almost two-thirds of its inhabitants.*

Langer further reports that

It is now estimated that the total population of England fell from about 3.8 million to 2.1 million in the period from 1348 to 1373. In France, where the loss of life was increased by the Hundred Years War, the fall in population was even more precipitate. In western and central Europe as a whole the mortality was so great that it took nearly two centuries for the population level of 1348 to be regained.

In many areas, the population did not return to its pre-plague level until

*This excerpt from *The Black Death* by William L. Langer. Copyright © 1964 by *Scientific American, Inc.* Reprinted by permission of W. H. Freeman and Company for *Scientific American.*

500 years later. The tragic extent of the epidemic was largely a result of the totally inadequate state of medical knowledge. The only treatments were bleeding, or the smelling or eating of aromatic herbs and unusual foods.

Because of the scarcity of carefully prepared histories of the fourteenth century, it is impossible to determine in detail the effects of the disaster. Clearly, the most profound aftermath was the deep impression the epidemic left on the people. The disease often dragged its victims through days of intense suffering, accompanied by extensive vomiting and a pervading stench surrounding the victim. When the bubons broke, black blood was discharged and the patient often died lying in a pool of the liquid. With an average of two people per household affected, few individuals in Europe escaped without direct contact with the plague.

How to Read an Annual Report* by Jane Bryant Quinn

To some business people I know, curling up with a good annual report is almost more exciting than getting lost in John le Carré's latest spy thriller.

But to you it might be another story. "Who needs that?" I can hear you ask. *You* do—if you're going to gamble any of your future *working* for a company, *investing* in it, or *selling to it.*

Why should you bother?

Say you've got a job interview at Galactic Industries. Well, what does the company do? Does its future look good? Or will the next recession leave your part of the business on the beach?

Or say you're thinking of investing your own hard-earned money in its stock. Sales are up. But are its profits getting better or worse?

Or say you're going to supply it with a lot of parts. Should you extend Galactic plenty of credit or keep it on a short leash?

How to get one

You'll find answers in its annual report. Where do you find *that?* Your library should have the annual reports of nearby companies plus leading national ones. It also has listings of companies' financial officers and their addresses so you can write for annual reports.

So now Galactic Industries' latest annual report is sitting in front of you ready to be cracked. How do you crack it?

Where do we start? *Not* at the front. At the *back!* We don't want to be surprised at the end of *this* story.

---

*From the Power of the Printed Word series, courtesy of International Paper Company.

Start at the back

First, turn back to the report of the *certified public accountant*. This third-party auditor will tell you right off the bat if Galactic's report conforms with "generally accepted accounting principles."

Watch out for the words "subject to." They mean the financial report is clean *only* if you take the company's word about a particular piece of business, and the accountant isn't sure you should. Doubts like this are usually settled behind closed doors. When a "subject to" makes it into the annual report, it could mean trouble.

What else should you know before you check the numbers?

Stay in the back of the book and go to the *footnotes*. Yep! The whole profits story is sometimes in the footnotes.

Are earnings down? If it's only because of a change in accounting, maybe that's good! The company owes less tax and has more money in its pocket. Are earnings up? Maybe that's bad. They may be up because of a special windfall that won't happen again next year. The footnotes know.

For what happened and why

Now turn to the *letter from the chairman*. Usually addressed "to our stockholders," it's up front, and *should* be in more ways than one. The chairman's tone reflects the personality, the well-being of his company.

In his letter he should tell you how his company fared this year. But more important, he should tell you *why*. Keep an eye out for sentences that start with "Except for. . ." and "Despite the. . ." They're clues to problems.

Insights into the future

On the positive side, a chairman's letter should give you insights into the company's future and its *stance* on economic or political trends that may affect it.

While you're up front, look for what's new in each line of business. Is management getting the company in good shape to weather the tough and competitive 1980's?

Now—and no sooner—should you dig into the numbers!

One source is the *balance sheet*. It is a snapshot of how the company stands at a single point in time. On the left are *assets*—everything the company owns. Things that can quickly be turned into cash are *current assets*. On the right are *liabilities*—everything the company owes. Current *liabilities* are the debts due in one year, which are paid out of current assets.

The difference between current assets and current liabilities is *net work-*

ing capital, a key figure to watch from one annual (and quarterly) report to another. If working capital shrinks, it could mean trouble. One possibility: the company may not be able to keep dividends growing rapidly.

Look for growth here

Stockholders' equity is the difference between total assets and liabilities. It is the presumed dollar value of what stockholders own. You want it to grow.

Another important number to watch is *long-term debt*. High and rising debt, relative to equity, may be no problem for a growing business. But it shows weakness in a company that's leveling out. (More on that later.)

The second basic source of numbers is the *income statement*. It shows how much money Galactic made or lost over the year.

Most people look at one figure first. It's in the income statement at the bottom: *net earnings per share*. Watch out. It can fool you. Galactic's management could boost earnings by selling off a plant. Or by cutting the budget for research and advertising. (See the footnotes!) So don't be smug about net earnings until you've found out how they happened—and how they might happen next year.

Check net sales first

The number you *should* look at first in the income statement is *net sales*. Ask yourself: Are sales going *up at a faster rate* than the last time around? When sales increases start to slow, the company may be in trouble. Also ask: Have sales gone up faster than inflation? If not, the company's *real* sales may be behind. And ask yourself once more: Have sales gone down because the company is selling off a losing business? If so, profits may be soaring.

(I never promised you that figuring out an annual report was going to be easy!)

Get out your calculator

Another important thing to study today is the company's debt. Get out your pocket calculator, and turn to the balance sheet. Divide long-term liabilities by stockholders' equity. That's the *debt-to-equity ratio*.

A high ratio means that the company borrows a lot of money to spark its growth. That's okay—*if* sales grow, too, and *if* there's enough cash on hand to meet the payments. A company doing well on borrowed money can earn big profits for its stockholders. But if sales fall, watch out. The whole enterprise may slowly sink. Some companies can handle high ratios, others can't.

You have to compare

That brings up the most important thing of all: *One* annual report, *one* chairman's letter, *one* ratio won't tell you much. You have to compare. Is the company's debt-to-equity ratio better or worse than it used to be? Better or worse than the industry norms? Better or worse, after this recession, than it was after the last recession? In company-watching, *comparisons are all*. They tell you if management is staying on top of things.

Financial analysts work out many other ratios to tell them how the company is doing. You can learn more about them from books on the subject. Ask your librarian.

But one thing you will *never* learn from an annual report is how much to pay for a company's stock. Galactic may be running well. But if investors expected it to run better, the stock might fall. Or, Galactic could be slumping badly. But if investors see a better day tomorrow, the stock could rise.

Two important suggestions

Those are some basics for weighing a company's health from its annual report. But if you want to know *all* you can about a company, you need to do a little more homework. First, see what the business press has been saying about it over recent years. Again, ask your librarian.

Finally, you should keep up with what's going on in business, economics and politics here and around the world. All can—and will—affect you and the companies you're interested in.

Each year, companies give you more and more information in their annual reports. Profiting from that information is up to you. I hope you profit from *mine*.

12
APPLICATION: WRITING

Mapping and other techniques
to make writing clearer and more effective

Writing transmits throughts from one mind to another across time and distance. Good writing transmits the thoughts clearly, accurately, and with a regard for the readers' efforts.

Conventional writing courses and texts abound with techniques and advice to attain these goals. A few of the most basic techniques and guidelines are given here—they can help in the mechanical process of writing and in the quality of the product.

ORGANIZING WRITING

Good organization makes writing easier and clearer. A detailed plan lets you concentrate on writing faster and more purposefully. Systematic techniques for organizing and outlining are naturally more useful for articles and reports than for shorter memos and letters. Still, good organization is important for all expository writing—regardless of brevity.

You can reveal the organization of readings with thought maps. Maps show subordinate points radiating from the central core points in a graphic view of the material that is easy to understand and remember.

The mapping process can be reversed so that you begin with maps and develop the writing from them.

Much of the work is done by ordering points on index cards. First write all the points you want to make on the cards. (Index cards are available at stationery stores.) Assign one point to a card. Recognize that the points on the cards are notes to yourself—do not spend much time or energy turning them into acceptable prose. That comes later.

Separate the cards into groups of closely related points. Cards for an article about vitamins, for example, are grouped so that points about vitamin C are separated from points about vitamin E, and so on. Now order the points within each group in the most logical sequence, so that one point ushers in the next. When the points are not logically connected, order them according to their importance. The most important point is usually put first. However, when you are building an argument or seeking a dramatic effect, reverse the order to culminate with the most important point.

Each group of cards now corresponds to a core point, and the individual cards correspond to the various subordinate points. Write the core point on a covering card for each group of cards. This step encourages you to see your writing in broad central points. Writing is more coherent with such core points in mind, and transitions are helped by referring to the core point. Suppose, for example, that a core label is "Stock Growth Indicators." The section might begin "Stock growth is indicated by several numbers . . .," and later paragraphs might open with "Another number . . ." and "Growth is also reflected by. . . ." Throughout the section, the unity and flow of the writing is helped by occasional references to the core point.

Finally, organize the core points. These too can be ordered according to a logical sequence or order of importance. The ordered pile of cards is your outline. Translate the outline into thought maps to get a visual perspective of the whole unit. The time you spend organizing will be repaid generously during the writing process.

THE MECHANICS OF WRITING

Editing is easier than writing. Much easier. This is a key fact to consider in writing a rough draft.

Write a rough draft rapidly from your maps and cards. Try to get the whole story told with little concern for phrasing, transitions, or brevity. Do not struggle with fine points of clear writing—after all, you are going to rewrite. It can be difficult to write quickly; only a few writers fly through the rough draft, while others can rise only to glacial rates.

New ideas often flash into mind as you write. Record them. Revisions in organization may also suggest themselves. If they are good, incorporate them. Some specialists believe you should formulate all your thoughts during the writing process; in their view, a rough draft should be written *before* the outline. My approach is more conventional, but flexible enough to allow you to incorporate new ideas and structural changes during writing.

Write the introduction last. An introduction can serve various purposes: (1) to orient the reader to the subject and its value, using historical, anecdotal, and factual background; (2) to stimulate interest in the subject; (3) to state the purpose of the writing; (4) to summarize results, conclusions, or recommendations; (5) to announce the plan of the material. The introduction to a chapter or section may use only one or two of these elements, while the introduction to a full report or article may include them all. In every case, writing the introduction is easier after the body has been developed.

When you complete the rough draft, put it away for a day or two so that you can read it more objectively. Then revise it.

The revision should have acceptable phrasing and transitions and should meet the guidelines for clear writing described in the following section. Simply put, it should be a readable manuscript. Many writers edit several more times, but it is rare for good writers to do without one revision. Even Isaac Asimov, one of the most prolific expository writers in the world, takes the time to do a rewrite.

WRITING FOR THE READER

Most readers want direct, informative articles that are free of jargon and pomp. Readers appreciate the use of simple past and present tenses, short paragraphs, and uncomplicated sentences. Expository writing can be entertaining, even occasionally poetic, and still hold to a spare, easy-reading style. These features are preferred because they save the readers' time and effort.

But there are important exceptions to this "easy-reading" style. Some nonfiction writing is meant to stimulate, persuade, or cause emotional responses. Some writings are part essay and part poetry. These forms presume the reader seeks more than naked ideas and information, and the author can enjoy more latitude to embroider with language.

An extreme is found in some technical writing that is filled with obscure terms and wordy, convoluted sentences. Often this is simply poor writing by specialists. Some disturbing studies suggest that muddy prose is being rewarded in college composition courses and that professionals tend to praise reports of work they do not understand. We need to recognize, however, that specialized legal, financial, medical, and academic articles need very accurate wording and that readers are willing to sacrifice time and effort for a bit more precision. Technical jargon has a proper place in such literature because it is easily understood by the specialist-readers.

Ideally, your writing level should match your readers' knowledge of the subject. If you are a specialist writing for specialists, you must write in the appropriate idiom. Writing for the general public is more difficult, because you cannot assume readers have your background—or interest—in the subject. You need to write at a level they can understand. Readers want information, not a show of the author's superior knowledge.

Moreover, while writers must reach out to readers, they should not reach down. Readers are intelligent beings and deserve not to be offended by condescension.

It comes to this: all writing attempts to communicate; good writing attempts to communicate with people.

STREAMLINING WRITING

Writing becomes clearer and easier to read when it is made simpler, less wordy, and more direct. Here I want to mention a few guidelines to help streamline writing.

Stick to your outline. Let the bones of your organization show through your writing. A clear outline, closely followed, is as much a map for your readers as for you.

Cut unnecessary words, phrases, and sentences. If the phrase or sentence does not amplify or improve your message, strike it out. Writer Kurt Vonnegut refers to this as having the "guts to cut." It does take guts to cut words that once sounded so pretty and right. Cut them for your readers' sake.

Any sentence that uses many words to express a small thought is a likely candidate for trimming. Example: "Good organization makes writing easier for the writer and clearer for the reader." I edited this to "Good organization makes writing easier and clearer."

Weak qualifying phrases are another widespread source of fat. Sentences read better without them: "As the portability of computers grows, the concept of education ~~as it applies to many skills~~ will change."

Words can be streamlined too. Plain, familiar words are easiest to read. This means you might replace "adhere" with "stick" and "ubiquitous" with "widespread." Of course, you won't always want to simplify vocabulary, but simplification usually helps the reader direct attention to the message rather than to the words.

13
ON NOTES

Note taking
and studying from notes

A "notebook check" was a terrifying event. My teacher walked around the classroom and leafed through the students' notebooks, each as elegant and thick as a bible. I could hear my pulse as she approached my desk and the sloppy, scant scribble in my notebook. At last she was standing over me writing "unsatisfactory" everywhere and lecturing that a sloppy notebook reflects a sloppy mind.

I accepted that judgment for decades, but now I believe my sketchy notes were better for their purpose than any of the glorious volumes my teachers adored. All notes are summaries of ideas and information; the style of your notes should fit the functions you want them to serve. Some people might want a detailed abstract, but you might prefer notes that are personal reminders of material already learned, or you may simply need a permanent record of names, numbers, and other details.

NOTES AS ABSTRACTS

Notes can be rewrites of the original subject matter. These are abstracts that are literate, neat, and complete—they can be read by anyone.

Such notes include the infamous reviews of classic literature often read by schoolchildren in lieu of the originals. How this practice is despised by teachers! Nevertheless, when factual information—as distinct from an appreciation of literature—is being demanded from students, this is the student's best alternative. Condensation-type notes can serve as an outline for a telescopic approach. When you can obtain condensations of any subject matter, it makes sense to review them first. For learning purposes, it is far better to read such notes than to write them.

Most people do strive to write ideal condensation-type notes and many, including my former classmates, succeed admirably. The problem is that it is very difficult to write extensive notes and learn at the same time.

Watch a busy note-taker at a lecture; you can almost see the information passing into the ear, down the arm, and onto the paper without ever touching the brain. If learning could be insured by simply recording information, shorthand would be an essential skill.

TAKING NOTES

Of course, it is important to make permanent records of information that you cannot trust to memory or that is useless or burdensome to memorize. An effective note-taking format will help you keep such records without excessive transcription. In previous chapters you used thought maps to take notes from readings. Thought maps also work for most other vehicles of information, including lectures, presentations, and nonprint media.

The structure of thought maps assists learning and remembering. The core of each map is a central idea or fact represented by key words. (Listening or reading for central ideas demands close attention; it is a forced learning process.) Subordinate information radiates from the cores in a picturesque fashion, and the maps become more effective when they are embellished with sketches, designs, and coloring. Try these touches and see if they suit you. Keep the maps compact and visually simple—a liberal use of abbreviations will help.

Notes taken when listening and viewing are likely to be brief because time is limited by the rate of the presentation. Since more time is available when taking notes from printed matter, some readers will rewrite or highlight extensive passages. Resist this tedious practice.

Certainly the process of writing information, together with hearing or seeing it, helps us to learn. This is particularly true of vocabulary, terminology, and the like. Facts and ideas, however, are learned more efficiently when they are summarized as succinctly as possible.

Your goal should be to learn and take notes simultaneously. This requires that you trust your ability to reconstruct the full information from thought maps. It helps to let your confidence evolve by first writing maps that are almost as complete as the notes you now take. You can gradually make them briefer by relying more on key words and less on exposition. Most students proceed this way before they become adept at mapping.

Be aware that note-taking is seldom a precision process. Not every core point is easily recognizable, with the subordinate points clearly organized around the core. This is the ideal, but all too often the importance of various points is not clear until later. Record any questionable points in a conventional form. When you review these notes you can reconstruct them in visual map form. Temporarily discard the map format whenever it doesn't seem to fit the information—mapping should assist and not restrict you.

STUDYING NOTES

Review your notes as soon as possible. This insures that you will remember the meanings of your key words and terse personal messages. The review does not need to be a deep study. Simply check that you can reconstruct the information from the notes. Write short explanations for items that seem too cryptic. This is likely to be enough study for some subject matter.

When you study more difficult material, it helps to distill it with repeated reductions. You then have a layered view of the information, so that one level reminds you of the next in a cascade of associations—the telescopic approach. Memorization can be carried to any desired level by the procedures described below.

Information cast in thought maps is already reduced and easily remembered. Within each topic unit, say a chapter, the cores of the maps can be linked in a memory chain. This is enough to remember the basics. Many details are likely to be recalled from the cores after a simple review.

Complete maps can be memorized by treating them as branched lists where any item may have several others linked to it. The memory chain technique works nicely for branched lists. For instance, if the key word *hammer* is simultaneously linked to *beer, bell,* and *pudding,* you can easily visualize multiple associations to recall this linkage.

The full procedure, therefore, is to memorize core points with a memory chain, and then treat each core point as the first item in a branched list. As usual, use vivid substitute images and imaginative associations.

Exercises

1. The thought maps in Figure 13.1 describe the organization of a stage play. Use the procedure of this section to memorize and reproduce these maps. (It is not necessary to understand the maps to do this exercise. Naturally, it is easier to remember a meaningful map you developed yourself.)

FIGURE 13.1.

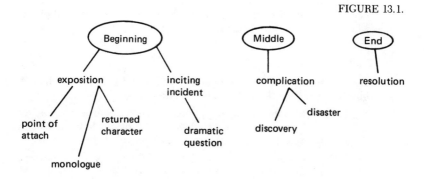

2. Memorize and reproduce the thought maps you developed for the reading exercises at the end of the last chapter.

SUMMARY

Notes as Abstracts: Writing extensive, literate condensations of information can impede learning.

Taking Notes: A thought-map format for notes assists learning and remembering. A compact but interesting map structure is best; use abbreviations and visual embellishments. Gradually improve note-taking by relying more on key words and less on exposition.

Studying Notes: Thought-map notes are treated by telescoping. (1) The thought-map cores are linked in a memory chain. (2) Subordinate items are linked to the cores in branched memory chains.

Exercise

Develop and memorize thought maps for the following readings. See whether you can think through all the important points—or, if you can find a very patient ear, deliver a detailed monologue.

How to Write a Resume* by Jerrold G. Simon, Ed.D.

If you are about to launch a search for a job, the suggestions I offer here can help you whether or not you have a high school or college diploma, whether you are just starting out or changing your job or career in midstream.

"What do I want to do?"

Before you try to find a job opening, you have to answer the hardest question of your working life: "What do I want to do?" Here's a good way.

Sit down with a piece of paper and don't get up till you've listed all the things you're proud to have accomplished. Your list might include being head of a fund-raising campaign, or acting a juicy role in the senior play.

Study the list. You'll see a pattern emerge of the things you do best and like to do best. You might discover that you're happiest working with people, or maybe with numbers, or words, or well, you'll see it.

Once you've decided what job area to go after, read more about it in the reference section of your library. "Talk shop" with any people you know in that field. Then start to get your resume together.

There are many good books that offer sample resumes and describe widely used formats. The one that is still most popular, the *reverse chronological*, emphasizes where you worked and when, and the jobs and titles you held.

---

*From The Power of the Printed Word series, courtesy of International Paper Company.

How to organize it

Your name and address go at the top. Also phone number.

What job do you want? That's what a prospective employer looks for first. If you know exactly, list that next under *Job Objective*. Otherwise, save it for your cover letter (I describe that later), when you're writing for a specific job to a specific person. In any case, make sure your resume focuses on the kind of work you can do and want to do.

Now comes *Work Experience*. Here's where you list your qualifications. *Lead with your most important credentials.* If you've had a distinguished work history in an area related to the job you're seeking, lead off with that. If your education will impress the prospective employer more, start off with that.

Begin with your most recent experience first and work backwards. Include your titles or positions held. And list the years.

Figures don't brag

The most qualified people don't always get the job. It goes to the person who presents himself most persuasively in person and on paper.

So don't just list where you were and what you did. This is your chance to tell *how well you did.* Were you the best salesman? Did you cut operating costs? Give numbers, statistics, percentages, increases in sales or profits.

No job experience?

In that case, list your summer jobs, extracurricular school activities, honors, awards. Choose the activities that will enhance your qualifications for the job.

Next list your *Education*—unless you choose to start with that. This should also be in reverse chronological order. List your high school only if you didn't go on to college. Include college degree, postgraduate degrees, dates conferred, major and minor courses you took that help qualify you for the job you want.

Also, did you pay your own way? Earn scholarships or fellowships? Those are impressive accomplishments.

No diplomas or degrees?

Then tell about your education: special training programs or courses that can qualify you. Describe outside activities that reveal your talents and abilities. Did you sell the most tickets to the annual charity musical? Did you take your motorcycle engine apart and put it back together so it works? These can help you.

Next, list any *Military Service.* This could lead off your resume if it is your only work experience. Stress skills learned, promotions earned, leadership shown.

Now comes *Personal Data*. This is your chance to let the reader get a glimpse of the personal you, and to further the image you've worked to project in the preceding sections. For example, if you're after a job in computer programming, and you enjoy playing chess, mention it.

Chess playing requires the ability to think through a problem.

Include foreign languages spoken, extensive travel, particular interests or professional memberships, *if* they advance your cause.

Keep your writing style simple. Be brief. Start sentences with impressive action verbs: "Created," "Designed," "Achieved," "Caused."

No typos, please

Make sure your grammar and spelling are correct. And no typos!

Use 8½″ x 11″ bond paper—white or off-white for easy reading. Don't cram things together.

Make sure your original is clean and readable. Then have it professionally duplicated. No carbons.

Get it into the right hands

Now that your resume is ready, start to track down job openings. How? Look up business friends, personal friends, neighbors, your minister, your college alumni association, professional services. Keep up with trade publications, and read help-wanted ads.

And start your own "direct mail" campaign. First, find out about the companies you are interested in—their size, location, what they make, their competition, their advertising, their prospects. Get their annual report—and read it.

No "Dear Sir" letters

Send your resume, along with a cover letter, to a specific person in the company, not to "Gentlemen" or "Dear Sir." The person should be the top person in the area where you want to work. Spell his name properly! The cover letter should appeal to your reader's own needs. What's in it for him?

Quickly explain why you are approaching *his* company (their product line, their superior training program) and what you can bring to the party. Back up your claims with facts. Then refer him to your enclosed resume and ask for an interview.

Oh, boy! An interview!

And now you've got an interview! Be sure to call the day before to confirm it. Meantime, *prepare yourself*. Research the company and the job by reading books and business journals in the library.

On the big day, arrive 15 minutes early. Act calm, even though, if you're normal, you're trembling inside at 6.5 on the Richter scale. At every chance, let your interviewer see that your personal skills and qualifications relate to the job at hand. If it's a sales position, for example, go all out to show how articulate and persuasive you are.

Afterwards, follow through with a brief thank-you note. This is a fine opportunity to restate your qualifications and add any important points you didn't get a chance to bring up during the interview.

Keep good records

Keep a list of prospects. List the dates you contacted them, when they replied, what was said.

And remember, someone out there is looking for someone *just like you*. It takes hard work and sometimes luck to find that person. Keep at it and you'll succeed.

*Physics' Newest Frontier**

The universe, astronomers have found, is expanding, the clusters of galaxies hurtling away from one another. Run the expansion backward, physicists reason, and you come to a time some 20 billion years ago when everything must have been mashed together in a state of titanic heat and density. The molecules, atoms and nuclei of atoms into which we find matter organized today could no more have existed in the primordial fireball than a set of crystal wineglasses could survive being dropped into the sun. Therefore the complex structures characteristic of matter today must have evolved later on, as the universe expanded and cooled.

The unified theories hold that the four interactions now at work in nature could have evolved from three, two or just one interaction that held sway when the universe was very young. When combined with cosmology, the theories become a tale of cosmic history that portrays today's natural laws as the children of simpler, primordial laws—or law.

If the structure of matter and the principles that govern its behavior reveal information about the early history of the cosmos, then the history of the universe can be read in every scrap of matter, everywhere. Each atom could be viewed as a storehouse of historical information, able to tell us about the universal past much as geological strata tell us about the history of the earth.

The idea that physics can probe cosmic history was first glimpsed decades ago by astrophysicists, the scientists who apply physics to the study of the

---

*From "Physics' Newest Frontier," by Timothy Ferris, *New York Times Magazine*, September 26, 1982. © 1982 by The New York Times Company. Reprinted by permission.

stars. In studying the composition of the stars and interstellar clouds, they found evidence that whole galaxies act as engines of chemical evolution, building simple atoms into more complicated atoms within the stars, then returning the complex atoms into the interstellar clouds when each star explodes. They determined that our sun and its planets formed from the condensation of a chemically enriched interstellar cloud rather recently—about five billion years ago—in the roughly 15-billion-year history of the Milky Way Galaxy, and that consequently we on earth have inherited an abundance of heavy atoms that were processed through stars that died before the sun was born.

Carbon atoms, upon which all terrestrial life is based, appear to have been built out of helium atoms in the cores of middle-sized stars that subsequently ran out of nuclear fuel and exploded, spewing the carbon and the other heavy atoms they had created into the surrounding interstellar medium. When the solar system condensed from the enriched interstellar clouds, it incorporated the heavy elements generated by the deceased stars. Atoms of the heavier elements, such as gold, required for their creation the furious energies generated when giant and supergiant stars explode as supernovae; the atoms in every nugget of gold on earth, the astrophysicists find, are pieces of stars that exploded before the solar system was created. Hydrogen—the "H" in the H_2O that makes up most of each human being—is much older; it was created in the cosmic fireball during the first minutes of the expansion of the universe. So too, it seems, was most helium. The helium atom in a child's carnival balloon holds atoms [which] were created when the universe was 2 minutes 15 seconds old.

These discoveries revealed that the history of the universe—or at least its history since the first moments of the big bang—is woven throughout the structure of matter. The physicist John Wheeler, whose work has inspired three generations of scientists, put it this way, in a lecture to the Smithsonian Institution and National Academy of Sciences: "The wood in a table is a 'fossil' from a photochemical reaction in a tree 20 years ago. Heat it—not very much—and its entire molecular constitution will change. The nuclei of iron in a watchband were created in a thermonuclear reaction in a star some billions of years ago at temperatures of 10 to 20 million degrees. It, too, is a fossil.

"Today," Wheeler said, "we find ourselves challenged to think of the 'elementary particles' that make up these molecules and nuclei as fossils also—fossils likewise subject to reprocessing, fossils from the most extreme conditions of all, at the big bang itself."

Traditionally, physicists searching for a unified theory sought an ultimate particle out of which all the others were made. Once it had seemed that atoms were the fundamental building blocks. But atoms proved to be composed of smaller particles—protons, neutrons and electrons—and the protons and neutrons turned out to incorporate clouds of particles called mesons, and there are several sorts of mesons, each evidently composed of still smaller particles that scientists have named "quarks" (from a word coined by James Joyce in "Finnegan's Wake"). Today, the world of subatomic particles soon became as jumbled as an acquisitor's attic. Today the count of particles whose traces have been detected by ever more sophisticated accelerators, or whose existence has been postulated by physicists' calculations, extends to more than 200, so many that physicists are obliged to consult the 120-page Particle Properties Data Booklet just to keep track of their names and characteristics.

The reigning scheme for discerning—or imposing—order among the particles is the theory of quarks, conceived independently in 1963 by Murray Gell-Mann and by George Zweig, both of Caltech. Viewed from the perspective of this theory, particles can be categorized as either leptons or hadrons. The leptons (from the Greek for "light") which have no perceptible internal structure include electrons, muons, tauons, and neutrinos. The hadrons (from the Greek for "stout") include protons, neutrons, pions, kaons and a host of other particles, all thought to be composed of quarks. (Six varieties of quarks are now postulated. In order of ascending mass these are the "up," "down," "strange," "charmed," "bottom" and "top" quarks.)

14
THE BRAIN

Learning and the structure,
function, and feeding of the brain

This chapter is devoted to some of the findings of a variety of disciplines that now are loosely termed "cognitive sciences." The amalgam includes theories and research in brain physiology, memory, artificial intelligence, problem-solving, nutrition and pharmacology, and educational psychology. *The Brainbooster* is a practical handbook of applied cognitive sciences.

BRAIN STRUCTURE

The human brain is the most complex device on this planet. It is a switchboard wired with some ten billion *neurons*, long slender cells that carry electrical impulses. Hundreds of fibrous branches, the *dendrites*, may radiate from the ends of a neuron, connecting it with other neurons in a dizzying network.

The interior portions of the brain govern the most primitive activities: the monitoring, coordination, and control of bodily processes and some basic emotions. Higher functions are invested in the outer portion of the brain, the *cortex*. The folds and convolutions of the cortex give the brain its familiar appearance of a huge grey walnut. A map of the cortex shows areas associated with vision, hearing, touch and muscle control, smell and taste, and language. It contains 75 percent of the brain's neurons, all of which must be fed by a rich blood supply. Somehow, in ways not yet understood, the cortex thinks and learns.

About 25 percent of the calories we consume are spent to fuel the brain. The laws of thermodynamics demand that systems must spend energy to organize and build structures. All life therefore expends energy to maintain its structure, but the brain devours energy some ten times faster than other tissues. This is a vast expenditure to support a vast organization, a dynamic structure of chemical changes, dancing electrical impulses, and enough conducting fibers to girdle the world four times.

Your brain improves with use and, with some care and some luck, it can be more powerful than ever with advancing years. Most of the brain's flexibility lies in the possibility of improving its "programming"—in a word, learning. Concepts and information are probably chemically inscribed in new patterns and pathways for electrical messages. Each new pattern may be associated with old patterns, so that prior learning makes new learning easier.

Rats developed a thicker, heavier cortex when they were given a rich environment of toys, ramps, wheels, and the like. Very likely a similar enrichment takes place in humans who continue throughout life with education and mental challenge. Ordinarily, the aging brain may suffer a minor loss of neurons and a decline of certain chemical quantities. It now seems likely that such declines can be more than compensated for by a vigorous intellectual life and with good nutrition and lifestyle. People engaged in creative and educational pursuits often continue their intellectual growth throughout life.

TWO BRAINS

Your brain is both a logician and an artist. The logician is the left hemisphere, the analytic computerlike half of your brain that speaks, does arithmetic, and analyzes problems step by step. The artist is the right hemisphere, the imaginative, creative, and visual half of your brain. This hemisphere organizes thoughts in patterns and sees things whole.

Some bold contrasts can be seen by comparing the functions of the logical left brain and the artistic right brain:

Left Brain	Right Brain
Thinking with words; vocabulary, reading, and writing.	*Thinking with images;* visualization, spacial relations, drawing.
Serial processing; step-by-step thinking, as in arithmetic.	*Simultaneous processing;* grasping things all at once, like recognizing faces.
Logical thinking.	*Intuitive thinking.*
Analysis; breaking things into components.	*Synthesis;* fusing components into an integrated whole.

Although each hemisphere dominates particular functions, the other hemisphere has similar abilities, but in weak form. People who have lost all speech due to a massive injury to the left hemisphere have, with therapy and fortitude, learned to speak again using the "mute" right hemisphere.

The hemispheres work together by sending messages back and forth through a bridge of nerves called the *corpus callosum.* When this is cut, the hand controlled by the left brain can write but not draw, whereas the other hand can draw but not write. Incidentally, the left hemisphere controls the right hand and vice versa; this does not appear related to left- or right-handedness.

Most schooling is aimed at the analytic left brain. Indeed, traditional education discourages right-brain functions—drawing and daydreaming are crimes in the classroom. The creative hemisphere is not treated as part of the intellect! This is less surprising when one realizes that we communicate with language, the currency of the left brain. The left brain then has a window to other minds, while the mute right brain labors in the lonely attic of imagination. Thus Shakespeare's plays and Einstein's theories were conceived by the right hemisphere and written by the left.

Unlike traditional schooling, learning techniques tap the immense resources of the right brain. The telescopic approach and the various mnemonic techniques depend upon organization, visualization, and association. Organization is a result of synthesis, of putting the parts together and seeing them as an integral whole. Visualization and visual associations are similarly right-hemisphere functions. Your deliberate efforts to use these principles in learning is akin to enlisting the help of an extra brain.

COMPONENTS OF MEMORY

Researchers recognize three components of memory: sensory, short-term, and long-term memories. Each has a distinctive role in capturing and storing information that we can use to further our efforts at remembering.

Sensory memory does not seem very much like a part of memory. It is a buffer that captures, for just a moment, all that you see, hear, and feel. Sensory memory holds an enormous amount of information, but only for a very short time (less than a second). You might glimpse a group of people and recognize a familiar face only after your eyes have left the scene. The scene had to be stored momentarily for your brain to perform this feat.

We capture information from sensory memory by focusing attention on it. This moves the sensory information into the conscious memory—the storage place of our current thoughts, our awareness. The conscious memory is brief, usually lasting only a few minutes under continual rehearsal. Because of this limited storage time, conscious memory is called *short-term memory* (although sensory memory is even shorter).

At any moment, short-term memory can hold about seven items, give or take two items. This means that you can telephone a seven-digit number immediately after hearing it, but not an unfamiliar ten-digit number. When you try to fill your short-term memory with excess items, some of the original items spill out. You may be interrupted after looking up a phone number, and the number flies from your mind.

The number of items in short-term memory is more important for remembering than is the information in these items. For example, the letters *C*, *P*, *S*, and the words *Cup*, *Pencil*, *Staple* are about equally easy to hold in conscious memory. Moreover, we are better able to remember the single word C_APS than the list C,P,S. This is one reason why acronyms are good mnemonic devices.

Other techniques also depend on the ability of conscious memory to hold condensed information in chunks. Numbers, for example, are best remembered in groups of three or four digits; this is called *chunking*. Each stage in the telescopic approach, from the broadest outline to the smallest cluster of details, should contain few enough elements to be held entirely in short-term memory. Moreover, key words are summary devices that hold a lot of information in a single chunk.

Long-term memory is the storehouse of the brain—the component we most associate with learning. Its capacity is enormous, and some researchers now believe that long-term memory is virtually permanent. They believe that forgetting is not due to fading memory traces. Rather, the traces may be "lost" because we cannot find where we stored them. Techniques based on association are powerful because they forge hooks to fish out stored information.

One major factor that affects the retention and retrieval of information in long-term memory is organization. Organization is so essential to learning that we *must* impose artificial structure on material that does not have a clear natural organization. Our telescopic techniques systematically impose organization whether it is natural or artificial.

A second major factor for long-term memory storage is rehearsal. Repeated rehearsal in short-term memory moves the information into long-term memory. Rehearsal also reduces the rapid forgetting caused by the "interference" of new information. Most of us discovered the use of rehearsal early in life and repeated things over and over till they burned their way into our memories. Rehearsal is almost synonymous with conventional study. It will always be a most important and reliable tool, but other learning techniques can help you to markedly reduce this tedious practice.

FEEDING THE BRAIN

Athletes take food supplements and follow special dietary regimens to enhance their performances and extend their careers. It now appears that mental athletes can do the same. Several nutrients and drugs have been found to improve and extend memory and learning in animals and humans.

Brain functions are profoundly affected by chemicals called *neuro-transmitters*, which carry signals from one neuron to another. There are about twenty-five known neurotransmitters, and at least five are directly influenced by specific nutrients in foods.

Acetylcholine is perhaps the most important neurotransmitter for memory and learning. An aged brain can suffer a sharp decline in its amount of acetylcholine—a deficiency that is implicated in some senility and in learning and memory disorders.

Fortunately, these particular disorders may be reversed by increasing the brain's acetylcholine with nutritional therapy. A nutrient called lecithin (phosphatidylcholine) is converted into the neurotransmitter by the body. Lecithin is a natural ingredient in many foods and is abundant in egg yolks, liver, and soybeans. Pure lecithin is available from chemical supply houses and, in less pure form, from health-food stores. (Look for "triple strength" or 35 percent phosphatidylcholine.)

Healthy young people also benefit from lecithin. One experiment showed clear memory improvement in subjects taking eighty grams per day. This is probably too much to take without medical supervision. Some proponents think that since lecithin is a natural foodstuff, there is no danger in taking too much. However, I know of one man who suffered from cramps after taking only a few grams. At present there is no consensus on how much lecithin is best for optimum results, so it is prudent to assume that this, and almost any nutrient, can be taken in excess.

A bonus: lecithin may lower the risk of arteriosclerosis and heart disease. Several studies found that lecithin supplements (of the order of twenty to forty grams a day) lowered cholesterol levels in a majority of high-cholesterol patients. The form of cholesterol most closely linked with heart disease, low-density lipoprotein, appears to be the form most affected by lecithin.

The related nutrient choline also promotes the formation of acetylcholine in the brain, and it too is available in health-food stores. Three grams daily is a substantial dose, but some people develop a fishy odor from this much choline. Lecithin is preferred for acetylcholine formation.

Another neurotransmitter important for learning and memory is norepinephrine. Its production in the brain is controlled by the amino acid tyrosine. Tyrosine is a natural component of protein, but it is the amount of tyrosine relative to other amino acids that is important for norepinephrine production. A small supplement of tyrosine may insure a favorable balance in the diet.

Medical research has demonstrated some remarkable effects of tyrosine on blood pressure. Tyrosine markedly lowers the blood pressure of hypertensive rats and raises the blood pressure of hypotensive rats to near normal levels. It is suspected, but not yet proven, that tyrosine extends a similar control over human blood pressure.

Tyrosine has yet another health benefit. Many psychiatrists believe that some cases of depression are due to inadequate norepinephrine neurotransmission. These should be helped by administering tyrosine. Indeed, preliminary studies confirmed that tyrosine has an antidepressant effect.

RNA, a natural component of foods, improves memory in experimental animals. It is found in high concentrations in seafood and can be obtained in supplement form (supplements should be above 12 percent RNA to be useful). A rough calculation based on animal studies suggests a dose of about 2 grams a day. However, RNA supplements must be used with caution. They should not be taken by people with kidney problems or gout (uric acid, a waste product of RNA metabolism, is the cause of gout). Moreover, RNA is acidic and can cause stomach upset. Production of RNA in brain neurons is stimulated by vitamin B_{12}. The vitamin increases learning rates in rats, and an estimated dose of 1000 micrograms per day has been suggested for learning improvement in humans.

Various drugs are also known to improve learning and memory, but these are likely to be less safe than nutrients. Drugs for learning and memory should not be taken over extended periods except as part of a program of medical treatment. Even then, the Food and Drug Administration does not approve the use of drugs to increase normal intelligence (although the same drugs are approved for other purposes).

15
MEMORY PEGS

A technique for rapid
and reliable mental storage of information

Ancient Greek orators gave long and detailed speeches without notes or cue cards. The speaker accomplished this by associating key ideas with objects in a house. The orator imagined himself walking through the house and, as each object arose in his mind, he recalled the corresponding phrase. Objects like doors, cabinets, and chairs served as mental pegs on which the orator could hang new images. This is an example of the memory peg technique, whereby you associate key images with familiar objects.

MEMORY PEGS

Almost any object can serve as a memory peg—a kind of mental file cabinet that stores information by association. Visualizable objects or scenes are directly associated with the peg items, but ideas and terminology are joined to the pegs as key words or substitute images. Try this exercise: For each item in the following list, make a vivid visual association with the object in the adjacent diagram. When you complete the associations, cover the word list but not the diagrams. Then see if you can recall the list from the diagrams alone.

Background	Key Words	Memory Peg
Dinosaurs and approximately 70 percent of all living species became extinct about 65 million years ago.	*Dinosaur dying* (suggestion: imagine a dying dinosaur smashing through the door)	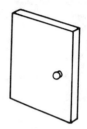
Many scientists believe the extinctions were caused by an asteroid that struck the earth.	*Asteroid* (suggestion: visualize a lamp-shaped asteroid plunging to earth)	
The asteroid crashed through the earth's crust and spewed huge clouds of dust and ash into the atmosphere.	*Dust and ash*	
The dust cloud surrounded the earth, blocking the sun for a few years.	*blocked sun*	

Widespread extinctions followed from: (1) world-wide cooking, and (2) plants dying for lack of sunlight. Animals that fed upon these plants soon followed, as did the meat-eating animals that preyed upon the plant-eaters.

worldwide cooling

plants died

Important evidence for the asteroid theory has been found in layers of rock. Generally, older rocks are deeper underground. Sixty-five-million-year-old rocks from around the world have been found to contain a thin layer of the element iridium, believed to be the fallout of the dust cloud. Iridium is not generally found on the surface of the earth, so the iridium deposit is thought to be due to the asteroid.

layers of rock

iridium
(suggestion: a red yam)

DEVELOPING YOUR OWN PEGS

You can now recognize some of the advantages of memory pegs over memory chains. It takes less time to make associations with familiar pegs than with items in a chain. Moreover, items can be easily recalled out of sequence, and you can safely forget various items without losing the whole list. Later I'll show that a combination of peg and chain techniques is most effective for applications like public speaking and remembering lectures and presentations.

An obvious drawback to the peg technique is that you must memorize peg lists. One sophisticated version of the peg technique uses numbers as pegs. This is a powerful approach because it imposes numerical order on the items, and the pegs are never exhausted. Nevertheless, this version takes considerable practice, and the extra benefit is probably not worth the extra effort. A numerical peg system is introduced in Chapter 20, but the system discussed here can be learned and used immediately.

I recommend an approach like that of the ancient Greek orators (sometimes referred to as the method of *loci*). Choose a room that is very familiar to you; perhaps a bedroom, kitchen, or office. Briefly review features and objects in the room in a definite sequence—perhaps starting with a door and working your way along the walls recording windows, decorations, and furniture along the way. Then you may spiral into the interior of the room, noting rugs, tables, chairs, lamps, etc. You must be able to visualize these pegs clearly, quickly, and in sequence.

Try to develop thirty or more pegs from one room. Use items that have somewhat permanent locations in the room. Do not use identical items in close proximity, like dining-room chairs or books on a shelf, because they can become indistinct in your memory. Rather, choose just one or two such identical objects and ignore the others.

Memory pegs can be used repeatedly to store different information. The pegs cannot be used twice in the same day, however, because the associations interfere with each other. Remarkably, the peg associations made a day apart seldom cause any confusion.

If you find later that you need more than one set of pegs, you can develop them from other rooms. The pegs can also be objects that you encounter on a familiar walk or ride. Shereshevskii placed list items along remembered routes—in a doorway, under a street lamp, against a fence. You will find, as he did, that it helps to exaggerate the pegs and associations. Even the illumination that you visualize is important because you can "overlook" an item like an egg in an unlit doorway.

You can also make useful peg lists from number rhymes. Variations of the following are most popular:

1	bun	6	sticks
2	shoe	7	heaven (picture clouds)
3	tree	8	gate
4	door	9	spine or twine
5	hive	10	hen

If you use this as a peg list, you can easily remember the numerical order of ten items.

Exercise

Most chemical properties of an element are determined by the atomic number of the atom (the number of orbiting electrons). Memorize the first ten elements according to their atomic number by associating their substitute images with the number rhyme above:

Atomic Number	Element	Suggested Substitute Image
1	hydrogen	hydrogen balloon
2	helium	heel
3	lithium	light thumb
4	beryllium	berries
5	boron	bore
6	carbon	powdered carbon, carbon paper
7	nitrogen	knight
8	oxygen	oxygen mask
9	fluorine	fluoridated water, floor
10	neon	neon lights

Now, without referring to the table, give the atomic numbers of the following elements: fluorine, carbon, neon, oxygen, beryllium, hydrogen, helium, lithium, nitrogen, boron.

USING PEGS

Memory pegs are most useful for rote-free learning and remembering, particularly for giving speeches and for absorbing lectures, presentations, films, and the like. These applications are presented in more detail in the next two chapters.

Of course pegs can also store information from readings. Most reading-to-remember should be recorded on thought maps because maps are permanent records in unlimited supply, unlike pegs. Still, the peg system is a convenient writing-free way to record uncomplicated readings. More importantly, using pegs for reading material is good practice for the other applications. Such exercises are given at the end of the chapter.

The most tidy and economical use of pegs is to attach core points to them. The subordinate points can then be linked to the cores by memory chains. The effect is to create a kind of thought map on each peg. These maps should be kept simple for applications requiring rapid memorization or recall. Elaborate maps take longer to decode.

SUMMARY

Memory Pegs: Almost any object can serve as a memory peg. When information is associated with these, they serve as mental file cabinets. The peg stimulates recall of the information.

Developing Pegs: Memory pegs are most easily formed from features and objects of a familiar room. It is desirable to develop about thirty pegs.

Memory pegs can be used repeatedly for different information. However, they *cannot* be used to record information twice on the same day.

Using Pegs: Associate core points with memory pegs, and link the subordinate points to these in memory chains.

Exercises

1. Check your recollection of about thirty pegs.

2. Without writing any notes, record the following articles on memory pegs. Check to see that you remember the main points.

How to Write with Style* by Kurt Vonnegut

Newspaper reporters and technical writers are trained to reveal almost nothing about themselves in their writings. This makes them freaks in the

*From The Power of the Printed Word series, courtesy of International Paper Company.

world of writers, since almost all of the other ink-stained wretches in that world reveal a lot about themselves to readers. We call these revelations, accidental and intentional, elements of style.

These revelations tell us as readers what sort of person it is with whom we are spending time. Does the writer sound ignorant or informed, stupid or bright, crooked or honest, humorless or playful—? And on and on.

Why should you examine your writing style with the idea of improving it? Do so as a mark of respect for your readers, whatever you're writing. If you scribble your thoughts any which way, your readers will surely feel that you care nothing about them. They will mark you down as an egomaniac or a chowderhead—or, worse, they will stop reading you.

The most damning revelation you can make about yourself is that you do not know what is interesting and what is not. Don't you yourself like or dislike writers mainly for what they choose to show you or make you think about? Did you ever admire an empty-headed writer for his or her mastery of the language? No.

So your own winning style must begin with ideas in your head.

1. Find a subject you care about

Find a subject you care about and which you in your heart feel others should care about. It is this genuine caring, and not your games with language, which will be the most compelling and seductive element in your style.

I am not urging you to write a novel, by the way—although I would not be sorry if you wrote one, provided you genuinely cared about something. A petition to the mayor about a pothole in front of your house or a love letter to the girl next door will do.

2. Do not ramble, though

I won't ramble on about that.

3. Keep it simple

As for your use of language: Remember that two great masters of language, William Shakespeare and James Joyce, wrote sentences which were almost childlike when their subjects were most profound. "To be or not to be?" asks Shakespeare's Hamlet. The longest word is three letters long. Joyce, when he was frisky, could put together a sentence as intricate and as glittering as a necklace for Cleopatra, but my favorite sentence in his short story "Eveline" is this one: "She was tired." At that point in the story, no other words could break the heart of a reader as those three words do.

Simplicity of language is not only reputable, but perhaps even sacred. The *Bible* opens with a sentence well within the writing skills of a lively fourteen-year-old: "In the beginning God created the heaven and the earth."

4. Have the guts to cut

It may be that you, too, are capable of making necklaces for Cleopatra, so to speak. But your eloquence should be the servant of the ideas in your head. Your rule might be this: If a sentence, no matter how excellent, does not illuminate your subject in some new and useful way, scratch it out.

5. Sound like yourself

The writing style which is most natural for you is bound to echo the speech you heard when a child. English was the novelist Joseph Conrad's third language, and much that seems piquant in his use of English was no doubt colored by his first language, which was Polish. And lucky indeed is the writer who has grown up in Ireland, for the English spoken there is so amusing and musical. I myself grew up in Indianapolis, where common speech sounds like a band saw cutting galvanized tin, and employs a vocabulary as unornamental as a monkey wrench.

In some of the more remote hollows of Appalachia, children still grow up hearing songs and locutions of Elizabethan times. Yes, and many Americans grow up hearing a language other than English, or an English dialect a majority of Americans cannot understand.

All these varieties of speech are beautiful, just as the varieties of butterflies are beautiful. No matter what your first language, you should treasure it all your life. If it happens not to be standard English, and if it shows itself when you write standard English, the result is usually delightful, like a very pretty girl with one eye that is green and one that is blue.

I myself find that I trust my own writing most, and others seem to trust it most, too, when I sound most like a person from Indianapolis, which is what I am. What alternatives do I have? The one most vehemently recommended by teachers has no doubt been pressed on you, as well: to write like cultivated Englishmen of a century or more ago.

6. Say what you mean to say

I used to be exasperated by such teachers, but am no more. I understand now that all those antique essays and stories with which I was to compare my own work were not magnificent for their datedness or foreignness, but for saying precisely what their authors meant them to say. My teachers wished me to write accurately, always selecting the most effective words, and relating the words to one another unambiguously, rigidly, like parts of a machine. The teachers did not want to turn me into an Englishman after all. They hoped that I would become understandable—and therefore understood. And there went my dream of doing with words what Pablo Picasso did with paint or what any number of jazz idols did with music. If I broke all the rules of punctuation, had words mean whatever I wanted them to mean, and strung them together higgledy-piggledy, I would simply not be understood. So you, too, had better avoid Picasso-style or jazz-style writing, if you have something worth saying and wish to be understood.

Readers want our pages to look very much like pages they have seen before. Why? This is because they themselves have a tough job to do, and they need all the help they can get from us.

7. Pity the readers

They have to identify thousands of little marks on paper, and make sense of them immediately. They have to *read*, an art so difficult that most people don't really master it even after having studied it all through grade school and high school—twelve long years.

So this discussion must finally acknowledge that our stylistic options as writers are neither numerous nor glamorous, since our readers are bound to be such imperfect artists. Our audience requires us to be sympathetic and patient teachers, ever willing to simplify and clarify—whereas we would rather soar high above the crowd, singing like nightingales.

That is the bad news. The good news is that we Americans are governed under a unique Constitution, which allows us to write whatever we please without fear of punishment. So the most meaningful aspect of our styles, which is what we choose to write about, is utterly unlimited.

8. For really detailed advice

For a discussion of literary style in a narrower sense, in a more technical sense, I commend to your attention *The Elements of Style*, by William Strunk, Jr., and E. B. White (Macmillan, 1970). E. B. White is, of course, one of the most admirable literary stylists this country has so far produced.

You should realize, too, that no one would care how well or badly Mr. White expressed himself, if he did not have perfectly enchanting things to say.

How to Write a Business Letter by Malcolm Forbes

A good business letter can get you a job interview.

Get you off the hook.

Or get you money.

It's totally asinine to blow your chances of getting *whatever* you want—with a business letter that turns people off instead of turning them on.

*From The Power of the Printed Word series, courtesy of International Paper Company.

The best place to learn to write is in school. If you're still there, pick your teachers' brains.

If not, big deal. I learned to ride a motorcycle at 50 and fly balloons at 52. It's never too late to learn.

Over 10,000 business letters come across my desk every year. They seem to fall into three categories: stultifying if not stupid, mundane (most of them), and first rate (rare). Here's the approach I've found that separates the winners from the losers (most of it's just good common sense)—it starts *before* you write your letter:

Know what you want

If you don't, write it down—in one sentence. "I want to get an interview within the next two weeks." That simple. List the major points you want to get across—it'll keep you on course.

If you're *answering* a letter, check the points that need answering and keep the letter in front of you while you write. This way you won't forget anything—*that* would cause another round of letters.

And for goodness' sake, answer promptly if you're going to answer at all. Don't sit on a letter—*that* invites the person on the other end to sit on whatever you want from *him*.

Plunge right in

Call him by name—not "Dear Sir, Madam, or Ms." "Dear Mr. Chrisanthopoulos"—and be sure to spell it right. That'll get him (thus, you) off to a good start.

(Usually, you can get his name just by phoning his company—or from a business directory in your nearest library.)

Tell what your letter is about in the first paragraph. One or two sentences. Don't keep your reader guessing or he might file your letter away—even before he finishes it.

In the round file.

If you're answering a letter, refer to the date it was written. So the reader won't waste time hunting for it.

People who read business letters are as human as thee and me. Reading a letter shouldn't be a chore—*reward* the reader for the time he gives you.

Write so he'll enjoy it

Write the entire letter from his point of view—what's in it for *him?* Beat him to the draw—surprise him by answering the questions and objections he might have.

Be positive—he'll be more receptive to what you have to say.

Be nice. Contrary to the cliche, genuinely nice guys most often finish first or very near it. I admit it's not easy when you've got a gripe. To be agreeable while disagreeing—that's an art.

Be natural—write the way you talk. Imagine him sitting in front of you—what would you *say* to him?

Business jargon too often is cold, stiff, unnatural.

Suppose I came up to you and said, "I acknowledge receipt of your letter and I beg to thank you." You'd think, "Huh? You're putting me on."

The acid test—read your letter *out loud* when you're done. You might get a shock—but you'll know for sure if it sounds natural.

Don't be cute or flippant. The reader won't take you seriously. This doesn't mean you've got to be dull. You prefer your letter to knock 'em dead rather than bore 'em to death.

Three points to remember:

Have a sense of humor. That's refreshing *anywhere*—a nice surprise in a business letter.

Be specific. If I tell you there's a new fuel that could save gasoline, you might not believe me. But suppose I tell you this:

"Gasohol"—10% alcohol, 90% gasoline—works as well as straight gasoline. Since you can make alcohol from grain or corn stalks, wood or wood waste, coal—even garbage, it's worth some real follow-through.

Now you've got something to sink your teeth into.

Lean heavier on nouns and verbs, lighter on adjectives. Use the active voice instead of the passive. Your writing will have more guts.

Which of these is stronger? Active voice: "I kicked out my money manager." Or, passive voice: "My money manager was kicked out by me." (By the way, neither is true. My son, Malcolm Jr., manages most Forbes money—he's a brilliant moneyman.)

Give it the best you've got

When you don't want something enough to make *the* effort, making *an* effort is a waste.

Make your letter look appetizing—or you'll strike out before you even get to bat. Type it—on good-quality 8½″ x 11″ stationery. Keep it neat. And use paragraphing that makes it easier to read.

Keep your letter short—to one page, if possible. Keep your paragraphs short. After all, who's going to benefit if your letter is quick and easy to read?

You.

For emphasis, *underline* important words. And sometimes indent sentences as well as paragraphs.

Like this. See how well it works? (But save it for something special.)

Make it perfect. No typos, no misspellings, no factual errors. If you're sloppy and let mistakes slip by, the person reading your letter will think you don't know better or don't care. Do you?

Be crystal clear. You won't get what you're after if your reader doesn't get the message.

Use good English. If you're still in school, take all the English and writing courses you can. The way you write and speak can really help—or *hurt*.

If you're not in school (even if you are), get the little 71-page gem by Strunk & White, *Elements of Style*. It's in paperback. It's fun to read and loaded with tips on good English and good writing.

Don't put on airs. Pretense invariably impresses only the pretender.

Don't exaggerate. Even once. Your reader will suspect everything else you write.

Distinguish opinions from facts. Your opinions may be the best in the world. But they're not gospel. You owe it to your reader to let him know which is which. He'll appreciate it and he'll admire you. The dumbest people I know are those who Know It All.

Be honest. It'll get you further in the long run. If you're not, you won't rest easy until you're found out. (The latter, not speaking from experience.)

Edit ruthlessly. Somebody ~~has~~ said that words are ~~a lot~~ like inflated money—the more ~~of them that~~ you use, the less each one ~~of them~~ is worth. ~~Right on~~. Go through your entire letter ~~just~~ as many times as it takes. ~~Search out and~~ Annihilate all unnecessary words, ~~and~~ sentences— even ~~entire~~ *paragraphs*.

Sum it up and get out

The last paragraph should tell the reader exactly what you want *him* to do—or what *you're* going to do. Short and sweet. "May I have an appointment? Next Monday, the 16th, I'll call your secretary to see when it'll be most convenient for you."

Close with something simple like, "Sincerely." And for heaven's sake sign legibly. The biggest ego trip I know is a completely illegible signature.

Good luck.

I hope you get what you're after.

Sincerely,

Malcolm Forbes

16
APPLICATION: SPEECHMAKING

Techniques for preparing and delivering
good speeches, lectures, and presentations

Public speaking has many forms. Reports across the conference table, formal speeches, lectures, and presentations all have their special styles and durations. In each case one vulnerable speaker addresses an audience of many. No other forum is as potent for instructing, influencing, and inspiring.

A few guidelines can help you to prepare and deliver effective talks. I focus on instructive lectures and presentations, but most of the discussion applies to any speech of twenty minutes or more. Brevity is an asset in almost any talk—try to keep your address under an hour. Even a highly interesting talk can turn sour when it runs too long.

Here I address four stages in the development and execution of a complete talk: organization, writing, practice, and delivery.

ORGANIZING THE TALK

The audience at your talk cannot reread passages for clarification. Once spoken, the information flies away at the speed of sound and dissipates. This is a problem because people need to organize, correlate, compare, and reorder information in order to learn. Superior speakers assume the burden of keeping organization and purpose before the audience, especially when the talk is technical.

A talk is divided into the *introduction*, the *main body*, and the *summation*. The introduction tells the audience what will be said; the main body says it; the summation tells what was said. Concentrate first on the organization of the main body.

Gather the material for your talk and write each of the points on a separate index card. Caution: it takes three or four times as long to deliver a talk as it does to read it; try not to include fine points that you will have to cut later due to time limitations. The cards are just notes to yourself, so do not bother to write them carefully for public address—yet.

Assemble the cards into small groups of closely related points—preferably less than six cards to a group. Order the cards within each group in either the most logical sequence or in ascending order of importance. Each group of cards now corresponds to a core point, and the cards within the group are subordinate points.

Label each card group with a covering core point card. Then order the core point groups either in the most logical sequence or in increasing order of importance. When the choice between these is not impelling, good rhetoric favors the ascending order of importance. The fully ordered pile of cards is your outline of the main body.

Make thought-map sketches from the outline. Each map should have a simple structure with few embellishments around the core. A talk needs to be simpler and easier to assimilate than written material because there is no opportunity to look back.

WRITING THE TALK

Write the main body of your talk from the maps and cards. Write as you would speak—not as you would write for an article. Keep your audience in mind throughout. How much do they know about the subject? How much detail can they digest in the limited time available? What is their interest in the subject? Do not aim for a level well above the audience's background—this sin can turn your talk into a lullaby. And if you simplify or popularize your topic, do so without condescension.

Experienced speakers may write very little and ad lib the rest. If you are new to the podium, you probably want to write every word of the speech. Write it on large index cards with each card reserved for one core point and its associated points. This format is easy to study and physically limits the amount of "clutter" surrounding any core point. Don't write too much—remember that a talk takes much longer to deliver than to read.

Now write the summation on one or two index cards. Briefly remind the audience of the highlights and theme of your talk. Make any projections or conclusions. Finish with a clear closing sentence or two. For example: "This concludes the discussion of cooperative quantum effects in chemical systems. Thank you very much," or "It's been a pleasure to speak to the Association today. Have a wonderful season."

The introduction is written last. It must orient the listeners to the subject and give the purpose and plan of the talk. Do so rather briefly and colorfully, if possible. An audience can lose interest quickly when the introduction is weak. Limit your writing of the introduction to three large index cards or less. Give a background discussion suitable for the level of the audience, reveal the purpose of the talk, and tell how you plan to do it. Mention the theme of the talk in words similar to those in the summation.

PRACTICING

A good speech sounds extemporaneous. Reading from notes erects a barrier between the speaker and audience with deadening effect. Many accomplished speakers *do* read prepared text, but their preparations are so thorough that the talk seems conversational and spontaneous—like that of an actor with memorized lines.

An address that is aired on radio or television must be scripted, because hesitations and awkward phrasings are magnified by these media. In other situations minor flaws actually make the talk more conversational and intimate. Regardless of the forum, talks are far more effective when they are memorized point by point. Veteran speakers avoid memorizing speeches word by word, because a practiced reading can give the same effect with much less effort. Exception: memorize the opening sentences in detail.

I recommend that you give speeches without notes. You can do this easily with the peg system; use one mental peg for every large index card. Prepare the pegs well enough to "read" them as you would cue cards. Even if you want written notes as a crutch, it helps your confidence and performance to have the points committed to memory.

Rehearse the speech until it is smooth. Time it without rushing, and trim when it is too long. On the other hand, a speech that successfully conveys your message cannot be too short.

ON STAGE

If you are new to the speakers' podium, you should expect to suffer some anxiety—stage fright. You have this in common with the very best speakers. Stage fright usually diminishes with experience, but it rarely disappears. Don't worry about it; it won't kill you, and the tension will probably sharpen your performance. Concentrate on doing the job rather than on your emotions. After you deliver the first few memorized lines, you will settle into a much more controlled state.

Face the audience as you would a gathering of good friends. Generally, the larger the audience, the more appreciative it is. Approval and applause are contagious, and the approval is amplified in a large group. Appear as relaxed as possible, and don't rush. A smile can start you in the right direction (but not while giving a eulogy). Your main concern, once you've begun, is to *talk to the audience*. Do not hide behind words—think about getting your message across. It helps to focus your attention on a few responsive people throughout the audience.

Brief anecdotes and humorous remarks are usually welcome in speeches. But beware of telling jokes—comedians are highly vulnerable speakers.

17
APPLICATION: LISTENING AND VIEWING

Mental recording of lectures,
TV shows, and motion pictures—without notes

Lecturers sometimes become captivated by their topics. I find myself pacing on the podium and waving my hands in a storm of ideas and equations. Suddenly, my fervor fizzles as I glimpse the audience writing hurriedly, without looking up. They never really listened to my zealous performance.

The problem is a familiar one. A speaker can lope along at a rate faster than 100 words per minute—several times faster than most people can write. Serious listeners feel that they cannot remember the outpouring of ideas, so they attempt to transcribe the information and learn it later. This is usually a difficult and a wasteful procedure because writing diverts attention from thinking. Even when the writing succeeds, the product is likely to appear unfamiliar.

Instead of transcribing presentations word by word, you can either take notes or memorize the central features in a kind of mental video-recording. Certainly note-taking requires less preparation and is more reliable because it produces a permanent record. Nevertheless, mental recording is an immediate and complete way to learn and remember. A permanent record can be made later upon rehearsing the material. Very likely you will find that you favor notes for some subjects and mental recordings for others. You can determine your preferences after some experimentation.

MENTAL RECORDING

Mental recording is an instrument for some impressive learning feats. Businesspeople use it to remember detailed presentations, students to absorb long lectures, viewers to relive their favorite motion pictures scene by scene—all after just one exposure and without formal study.

The basic idea in mental recording is to place important points on mental pegs. When the importance of a particular point is in doubt, it is stored on a peg to be on the safe side. The mental pegs you developed in Chapter 15 put you only minutes away from being able to remember a news broadcast or documentary film in detail.

Each important fact or idea is likely to have subordinate points. These embellishments are most comfortably attached by a memory chain to the same peg as the core point, rather than using new pegs. This is like storing a simple thought map on each peg.

This mixing of memory pegs and memory chains conserves the pegs and imposes organization on the material as you receive it. In practice, some information may not be packaged as you expect; then you can relinquish the ideal format and catch the items on pegs alone.

Exercise

Make a mental record of a thirty-minute news broadcast or information program. Do not be overly concerned about memorizing unfamiliar names or terms—these need special attention. Patiently reconstruct as much of the program as you can. Some pegs can be blank at first, but, as you review other information, you may be reminded of the "missing" information.

NAMES AND TERMINOLOGY
IN LISTENING

Mental recording is easy to do, with some exceptions. Unfamiliar names and terms are very difficult to digest from an outpouring of spoken words. The simplest solution is to write the names and terms. You can relate these to the appropriate pegs with only a modicum of concentration. Since most of my audiences are interested in techniques they can apply immediately, I recommend that they begin mental recording with a pen and paper backup.

Purists who insist on writing nothing must become proficient in using the substitute image technique rapidly. That is, they must first create a substitute image for a term and associate this with the appropriate peg. The procedure is familiar from memorizing readings, but the pace is dictated by the speaker. Keeping up takes plenty of practice.

ON LECTURES

The best feature of mental recording is that you can engage your mind rather than your pen. This does not apply to material that the speaker writes during a presentation, because you then have ample time for writing. I suggest that you transcribe most of what a lecturer writes, especially equations and diagrams. Of course, many experienced rapid learners take special pride in not writing anything—they put equations and diagrams on pegs. This is a showy demonstration, but it does require extra effort and is not absolutely necessary.

Lectures may be rich with information, so you should form associations only for information that is truly useful; this is important for reading recall, and essential for listening and viewing. Do not make special efforts to remember asides, embellishments, unessential details, or information that is familiar or obvious to you. New practitioners usually find they have abundant peripheral recall when they focus on central points.

As soon as possible, you should review the lecture and write it out in outline (thought maps are excellent for this purpose). You will find that this process is equivalent to hours of concentrated study by traditional methods.

A word of caution: do not rely on mental recording for important lectures until you have first practiced on several news or information programs. Even then, begin cautiously, with just one lecture per day. You can develop more pegs and handle more lectures as your ability and confidence grow.

VIEWING MEDIA

Note-taking cannot rival mental recording for remembering highly visual media presentations like motion pictures, stage shows, and television programs. For these the visual changes of scene are stronger cues than key words or even story lines.

A motion picture, for example, is most easily remembered by associating an exaggerated element from each scene with a memory peg. If a scene depicts people parachuting from a plane, then a vision of a tiny parachute would be a sufficient prod to remind you of the original scene. Remarkably, you may reconstruct an entire film so well that you notice connections or themes of which you were unaware in the actual viewing.

When information is somewhat dense, as it may be in an educational program, you must recall more than visual scenes. Usually it is quite sufficient to link memory chains of key images to the basic scenes. If there is too much detail in a scene to do this easily with a short chain, you are viewing a disguised lecture. Then simply forget about scenes as cues and concentrate completely on idea storage, as with any lecture.

SUMMARY

Mental Recording: To assimilate presentations, convert central ideas and facts to key images, and associate these with mental pegs. Attach subordinate points to the main point in a memory chain. Reconstruct the presentation patiently; seemingly blank spots will tend to fill in. Disregard unessential details and familiar or obvious information.

Names and Terminology: It is easiest to write down unfamiliar names and terms. Otherwise, replace terms with substitute images and link them to pegs.

On Lectures: Transcribe most material written by the lecturer, especially equations and diagrams.

Viewing Media: Visual media presentations are best absorbed by associating an exaggerated image from each scene with a peg.

Exercise

Practice mental recording of news broadcasts, motion pictures, and television presentations. (Do not use the same set of pegs more than once in a day.) When you are comfortable with the procedure, apply it to information-dense presentations and lectures.

18
S.O.S. FOR PROBLEM SOLVING

Techniques for solving verbal
problems in mathematics, science, and business

Professional problem solvers spend years building a mental arsenal of techniques that they summon unconsciously when the need arises. Certainly no single chapter can treat very many of these "trade secrets." There are, however, three basic procedures that can immediately transform your ability to solve typical verbal problems in mathematics, science, and business: Symbolize, Organize, Simplify—the S.O.S. approach.

Most experts don't know how they solve problems. Research indicates that they use a telescopic approach, where they first ignore details and impose a central principle. In applying the principle, they treat subordinate questions, each of which may cascade into smaller questions. (Diagrams of this expert problem solving then look like thought maps with a central principle as the core and the subordinate steps as the branches.) The S.O.S. techniques help you solve problems in the professional manner.

In this chapter, the reader is assumed to know elementary algebra. Work your way through; it takes plenty of practice to become adept at problem solving.

A most elementary form of problem solving is to substitute numbers into an equation. If a principal of P dollars is invested (at simple interest) at the yearly rate r, the yearly interest I is given by the equation

$$I = r P$$

This expression allows us to find any one of the three quantities, I, r, or P, from the other two. If, for instance, we know that interest is $240 and the rate is 12%, substitution in the equation gives

$$240 = .12P$$

and we find that the principal is $2000. Problems like this are so trivial that novice problem solvers can overlook the importance of writing information in symbol form in less obvious cases.

Many problems, for example, are solved with the help of some standard equations, but which equations are used in a given case? This may be answered most directly by writing a list of all symbols for the quantities in the problem. The symbol list will indicate which equations to apply.

We can illustrate this with a set of equations that describes the motion of an object with constant acceleration a (the acceleration of a body is the change in its velocity divided by the duration of the change—a kind of rate of a rate). Physics texts usually present three equations for this purpose:

$$x = v_0 t + \tfrac{1}{2} a t^2 \tag{1}$$

$$v = v_0 + at \tag{2}$$

$$v^2 = v_0^2 + 2ax \tag{3}$$

Here x is the distance (more precisely, the "displacement") through which the object moves, t is the time (duration) of the motion, v_0 is the initial velocity of the object, and v is the later velocity of the object (after moving a distance x in time t). The choice of the "proper" equation depends on the problem.

163

Example: An astronaut stands on the moon and throws a rock vertically upward. It rises 1.2 meters in 1 second. If the downward acceleration of all objects near the moon's surface is 1.6 meters/sec², what was the velocity of the rock at the point of release?

Solution: Use a convention where upward displacements, velocities, and accelerations are positive, and all are negative when downward. Now simply translate the verbal information into symbol form:

Statements	*Symbols*
rises 1.2 meters	$x = 1.2$ meter
in 1 second	$t = 1$ sec
downward acceleration . . .	$a = -1.6$ m/sec²
velocity at release	$v_0 = ?$

If possible, you want an equation that contains the unknown v_0, but no other unknown quantities. A glance at the symbol list for this example shows that equation (1) is the right choice. Substituting, we have

$$1.2 = v_0 (1) + \tfrac{1}{2}(-1.6)(1)^2,$$

with the result that v_0 is 2 meters/sec.

Exercise

A ball is thrown vertically upward at a velocity of 20 meters/sec and slows to 0.4 meters/sec after 2 seconds. Find the acceleration of the ball. *Answer:* -9.8 meters/sec². (Do not be concerned with units for the present.)

These straightforward problems show that symbolizing helps to identify the appropriate equation. In more difficult problems, the symbols also help to identify conditions needed to complete the problem. A list of the recognizable symbols can focus our attention on the "missing" symbols. These missing symbols correspond to conditions that are implied or assumed in the problem.

Example: A ball is thrown vertically upward at a velocity of 10 meters/ sec. What is the maximum height it attains above the point of release?

Solution: As before, we list the obvious symbolic information:

Statement	Symbol
thrown at a velocity	$v_0 = 10$ m/sec
maximum height . . .	$x = ?$

Certainly, this begs for more information if we are to use one of the three constant acceleration equations. These equations all contain acceleration a, so we must know or be given a value for a. Indeed, it is an important and surprising fact that all projectiles near the surface of the Earth have a downward acceleration of 9.8 m/sec²—whether they are rising or falling (assuming that air resistance is negligible). Our list now includes the value of a, but even this is not enough to solve the problem.

Equation (2) is not immediately useful because it does not contain the unknown, x. Equation (1) needs a value for t and Equation (3) needs a value for v in order to give a complete algebraic solution. Is either t or v related to the "maximum height" condition of the problem? Consider that the highest point reached by the ball is the point where it stops momentarily, so $v = 0$ (this is not so obvious, but it is true). The full list of symbols is now:

Statement	Symbol
thrown at velocity	$v_0 = 10$ m/sec
maximum height . . .	$x = ?$
fact: projectile acceleration	$a = -9.8$ m/sec
condition at highest point	$v = 0$

This symbol list leads us to substitute into equation (3), with the result that x is approximately 5.1 meters.

Exercise

A ball is thrown vertically upward at a velocity of 19.6 meters/sec. How long does it take to reach its highest point?
Answer 2 seconds.

Of course, not all problem conditions are numerical conditions like $v = 0$. Sometimes conditions are symbolic expressions like $L = 4W$. These can be included in symbol lists just like numerical data.

Example: The length of a rectangle is 4 times its width. The area is 100 cm. Find the width of the rectangle.

Solution: A general equation expresses the area A of a rectangle in terms of its length L and width W,

$$A = LW.$$

In order to solve for W, we need quantities or expressions for A and L. The list of symbols is:

Statement	*Symbol*	
length is 4 times width	L	$= 4W$
area is 100 cm	A	$= 100$ cm
find the width	W	$= ?$

Substituting into $A = LW$ gives

$$100 = 4W^2$$

with the solution $W = 5$ cm (and $L = 20$ cm). Notice that the only "new" step is to include a symbolic expression for L rather than a numerical value. Of course this simple problem can be done more directly, but the symbol-list approach works in more difficult cases too.

Exercise

The product of two positive numbers is 405, and one number is 5 times the other. Find the numbers. (Use the symbol-list approach of the last example.) *Answer:* 9 and 45.

In many problems you must bear in mind that N unknowns require N independent algebraic equations for their solution. Thus, the last example could have been treated by seeing it as a problem with two unknowns, W and L. Then we would write the two necessary equations as

$$A = LW$$
$$L = 4W,$$

with the symbol list $A = 100$, $W = ?$, $L = ?$. When you have a choice, it is usually easier to treat problems as having one basic equation, with any other symbolic expressions put in the symbol roster.

ORGANIZE

You should attempt to organize all but the most elementary problems. Write the relevant equations in full before substituting any numbers. Draw any diagrams that may help. Make a symbol list as in the last section. See the problem as a special case of a general principle, and try to treat it as such.

   Probably this advice is so obvious it seems trivial. But I believe that the greatest boost in problem-solving performance can come from a systematic approach to organization. When you first studied algebra, you learned to draw tables—tables for interest problems, tables for mixture problems, tables for age problems, ("If A is 12 years older than B was when C was twice as old as A will be. . . ."), etc. These tables organize particular types of problems very nicely, but unfortunately most of us have forgotten them. Worse, the tables are too specific—they do not show you how to organize new and unfamiliar problems. A more general approach to organizing problems is desired.

   Most verbal problems have a core equation, a central condition expressed in algebraic terms. This core equation can be used as the spine around which the problem solution is organized. In the sciences core equations are laws expressed in equation form. They are particularly easy to recognize from the problem statements; a constant acceleration problem, for example, is sure to have its core equation among the three equations of the last section.

   Some examples can show how various standard problems are organized around the core equation. The question that arises is which of several possible equations is a core equation. Almost any correct relation can serve as a core equation and can assist in problem organization, but the most useful expressions are usually the simplest, most obvious expressions.

Example: An investor with a $100,000 portfolio invests $40,000 at 6% and $35,000 at 8%. At what rate should the remainder be invested in order to yield a yearly interest of $7,000?

Solution: Although this is a simple problem, it illustrates the idea of a core equation. The most obvious relation is that the interest from three investments totals $7,000:

Interest A + Interest B + Interest C = 7,000.

This quite unspectacular expression can be used as a guide to write a symbol list:

Interest A = (rate) (principal) = (.06) (40,000)

Interest B = (.08) (35,000)

Interest C = (rate) (remainder) = r (25,000)

Now substitute these symbols into the core equation. A bit of algebra reveals r = .072 or 7.2%.

Exercise

A woman has $10,000 more invested at 7% than she has invested at 6%. Her annual income from these two investments is $2,000. How much is invested at 6%? (Use the core-equation approach.) *Answer* $10,000.

Example: A does a job in 45 minutes. A and B together do the same job in 20 minutes. How long would it take B alone to do the job?

Solution: The core condition here is that the work rates add together so that

Work rate A + Work rate B = Work rate together.

To see this clearly, think of a transparent case where a worker does one job per hour and another does two jobs per hour; working together, they do three jobs per hour. Similar additive equations apply to the rates of filling storage tanks or the rates of filling and emptying highways.

As usual, a symbol list is organized around the core equation:

$$\text{Work rate A} = 1 \text{ job}/45 \text{ min}$$
$$\text{Work rate B} = 1 \text{ job}/t \text{ min}$$
$$\text{Work rate together} = 1 \text{ job}/20 \text{ min}$$

Substituting these in the core equation and solving for unknown t gives $t = 36$ minutes.

Exercises

1. Three different pipes are used to fill a tank. Pipe A can fill it in 2 hours, pipe B in 3 hours, and pipe C in 6 hours. How long does it take for the three pipes together to fill the tank? *Answer:* 1 hour.

2. The storage tank of the last exercise develops a leak that can empty it in 4 hours. How long does it take to fill the tank with the three pipes and the leak? (Notice that the new rate subtracts from the rate of filling.) *Answer:* 1 hour, 20 minutes.

Example: How much 25% solution of acid should be mixed with 250 cc of 65% solution in order to obtain a 50% solution?

Solution: An equation that any mixture problem must satisfy is that the total material (acid in this case) is equal to the sum of material in all the parts. We can write

$$\text{Acid vol A} = \text{Acid vol B} = \text{Acid vol C}$$

This condition is indirect because the problem statement does not mention the volumes of acid, only the volumes of the acid solutions. Use the symbol V for the unknown volume of the 25% solution. Then the volume of acid in the solution is given by .25V. The symbol list is developed from the core condition and the problem information:

Acid vol A = .25V

Acid vol B = .65 (250)

Acid vol C = .5 (250 + V)

Substituting from the list into the core equation gives the result
V = 150cc.

Exercises

1. 320 kilograms of 45% copper alloy are to be mixed with an 85%
copper alloy to obtain a 60% alloy. How many kilograms of 85% alloy are
required? *Answer:* 192.

2. A confectioner has 6 kilograms of candy worth $4.00 per kilogram and
3 kilograms of another candy worth $5.00 per kilogram. How many
kilograms of a third candy at $2.00 per kilogram must be mixed with
these in order to have a mixture worth $3.50 per kilogram? (Notice that
the core equation here is that the total cost of the mixture equals the sum
of the costs of the components.) *Answer:* 5.

3. In a box of white balls and red balls, 8 more than half the total number
of balls are red and 6 more than half the number of red balls are white
balls. How many red balls does the box contain? *Answer:* 44.

When you use one core equation, write the symbol list in terms of
only one unknown (one equation, one unknown). Similarly, for two core
equations the list is written in terms of two unknowns, and so on. Part of
the organization process is to adjust symbol lists into the proper form.

Example: A rectangle has a width 1 less than the length, and its area is 2
more than the width squared. Find the width.

Solution: When the area, A, of a rectangle is involved, we expect that a
good core equation is the area equation:

$A = LW$

A first attempt at a symbol list gives the following:

Statement	Symbol
width 1 less than length	$W = L - 1$
Area 2 more than width squared	$A = W^2 + 2$

If we were to substitute this directly into the core equation, both L and W would appear in the result. To correct this, simply rewrite the symbol list so that only L or W appears to the right of the equal sign (but not both). Manipulating $W = L - 1$ in the symbol list gives a new list:

$$L = W + 1 \text{ (from } W = L - 1)$$
$$A = W^2 + 2$$

Now substitution in the core equation results in $W = 2$.

Exercise

The altitude of a triangle is 3 more than one-half the base, and its area is 30 less than the square of the altitude. Find the altitude and the area of the triangle. (Recall that the area of a triangle is one-half base times altitude.) *Answers:* 10, 70.

Another important step in problem organization is to draw diagrams and charts richly dressed with given information. The visual display often suggests core equations, and the labels help in formulating algebraic expressions.

Example: Car A leaves Los Angeles at 6 A.M. and travels at 60 miles per hour toward San Francisco, 400 miles away. Car B leaves San Francisco for Los Angeles and travels at 40 miles per hour. At what time do the cars pass each other?

Solution: A diagram (Figure 18.1) shows the distance between cities and the meeting point. The given information is all included in the diagram.

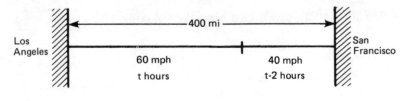

FIGURE 18.1.

In particular, the time elapsed after 6 A.M. is labeled t.

The core equation is obvious from the diagram:

Distance by A + Distance by B = 400 miles.

and the symbol list is equally evident from the labels:

Distance by $A = 60\,t$

Distance by $B = 40\,(t - 2)$

Substitution into the core equation gives $t = 4.8$ hours or 4 hours and 48 minutes. The cars meet at 10:48 A.M.

Exercise

A motorist drove 100 kilometers per hour on a country road and 60 kilometers per hour through town. A trip of 180 kilometers took 2 hours; how long was he traveling through town? *Answer:* One-half hour.

Yet another procedure for organizing a solution is to work backward. Imagine that you have the result, then ask yourself what step must immediately proceed it. If you can continue this process back to the beginning of the problem, the full solution is revealed. Working backward is especially useful for problems and puzzles that ask you to find a process to reach a desired goal.

Example: How can precisely 6 liters of water be measured with two containers, one with 9-liter capacity and the other with 4-liter capacity?

Solution: Let us draw the final situation first. This must be as follows:

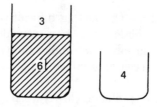

Immediately preceding this, the large container must have been full—after all, the only possible steps involve filling or emptying a vessel. In order for us to pour off only 3 liters, there must have been 1 liter in the small vessel:

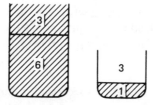

So now everything pivots on getting 1 liter of water in one of the containers. This is easily done by filling the smaller container from the large container twice:

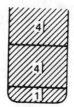

Now simply reverse the steps and the problem is solved.

Exercise

How can precisely 5 liters of water be measured with two containers, one with 7-liter capacity and the other with 3-liter capacity? (The answer will be clear when you find it.)

SIMPLIFY

Perhaps the best advice for treating difficult problems is to *solve a simpler problem*. The basic idea is to remove or simplify some of the equations until you can solve the simpler problem. Once the simpler problem is solved, you can reintroduce complications in steps until the full problem is done.

Solving-a-simpler-problem is heavy weaponry in problem solving. It is often the easiest, and sometimes the only, way to crack intransigent problems. The process usually takes too much time to use on exams, but its use ranges from difficult assignments to fundamental research problems.

Example: A streetsweeper charges C dollars for the first quarter of a mile and S dollars for each additional quarter of a mile. Write an expression for the charge (in dollars) to sweep a street of X miles (where X is greater than 1 mile).

Solution: This is solved with a succession of simpler problems.

Simpler Problem 1: Streetsweeper charges are S dollars for each mile. What is the charge for sweeping X miles:
Answer 1: SX.

Simpler Problem 2: Same as above but the charge is S dollars for each quarter mile.
Answer 2: $4SX$.

Original Problem: Now the charge for the first quarter mile is changed from S to C. Subtract S from the last answer and add C.
Answer: $C - S + 4 S X$

Exercise

Taxes are t dollars for every e dollars of income above \$3,000. Above \$60,000, income is taxed an additional 35%. Write an expression for the tax on an income of I dollars which is greater than \$60,000. *Answer:* $t(I-3,000)/e + .35(I-60,000)$.

Many kinds of problem elements can be simplified, including physical conditions, numbers, and the number of dimensions. A problem solver can find the speed of a cylinder as it rolls down a hill by first analyzing a cylinder that slides down the hill. Then it is obvious that the missing ingredient is rotational kinetic energy, and including this gives the full solution. Other problems may involve permutations and combinations (how many ways can ten students be assigned to twenty desks?). These become more transparent when the numbers are made small. In another case, the behavior of electrons in a crystal is understood by replacing the three-dimensional crystal with an artificial one-dimensional "periodic potential." Although these examples are too specialized to present in detail, they illustrate the wide applicability of solving-a-simpler-problem.

SUMMARY

Symbolize: Make a roster of symbols for all quantities in the problem. Symbols can be assigned numerical values or algebraic expressions. Use the roster to help determine the core equation—any central relation between the symbols.

Organize: Draw diagrams and write symbol lists. Organize solutions around a core equation. Undetermined symbols in the core condition are found from (1) a condition mentioned or implied in the problem statement or (2) from subordinate problems. When all quantities are expressed in terms of just one unknown, the problem is solved by substituting into the core equation.

Simplify: Reduce difficult problems to simpler ones that you can solve. Then add back the complexities in manageable stages.

19
APPLICATION: TEACHING WITH TECHNIQUES

The techniques for learning
and remembering as powerful teaching tools

Organization, visualization, and association accelerate learning and deepen memory—and the same principles can apply to teaching. In fact, several learning techniques can simply be inverted to create impressive teaching techniques.

Research findings in education, psychology, and brain physiology are far ahead of actual classroom practices. It is popular to blame this on the conservatism of the educational establishment. Yes, the system is conservative, but would we accept a teaching profession that readily embraces fads and untried methods? Most likely the gap between research findings and their application is due to the slow transmission of knowledge and a few erroneous views (discussed later) that keep us from fully using our new knowledge.

Many educators are eager to try promising innovations, especially when any failures can be easily corrected and the curriculum is not disrupted. These stipulations are met by the techniques described here; they are procedures that many enlightened teachers use routinely, without notice or fanfare.

As usual, I must paint a large subject with a broad brush. Professional educators have long been aware of much that follows, but I nevertheless want to mention the factors and procedures that, in my opinion, are the most important in good teaching. These methodologies also apply to teaching outside the classroom: teaching between parent and child, worker and coworker, professional and client.

THE HUMAN FACTOR

Human learning is profoundly influenced by personal factors. The most effective teachers give students respect, encouragement, and enthusiasm. Of course, it is easier to imagine that teaching is like programming a robot—that the information must be reduced to simple statements and fed into the student's empty brain. If teaching were simply this mechanical transmission of knowledge, virtually every knowledgeable person would be a good teacher. Sadly, this is not the case.

Your attitude is very important to your students, whether they are schoolchildren, coworkers, or clients. They want you to be approachable and genuinely concerned about them. Perhaps most of all, they want you to respect their abilities.

In a famous study, teachers were told that they had "bright" or "slow" students, although the classes actually were matched for equal abilities. Both groups were taught the same material and later tests confirmed that the "bright" students learned much more than the "slow" students. The labels were self-fulfilling.

The message is clear: when you genuinely respect your students, they share and meet your high expectations. Throughout this book I extol the human potential—and surely your own experience with learning techniques is evidence that we all have immense untapped resources. This is as true for the deprived and learning-handicapped as it is for gifted and talented individuals. Your students have impressive powers that deserve your admiration and respect.

Too many people regard praise and encouragement as peripheral or even extraneous to teaching. This is an understandable but mistaken view. There is a deep human need for approval, and it is a teaching tool you can use to great advantage. Conversely, try not to criticize students. Even when criticism is warranted, I believe it is counterproductive. Try to excuse or see something right about any wrong answer. If a student gives an incorrect answer for a "good" reason, acknowledge its virtue and correct it. At times you may have to suppress impatience, but the results are worth it.

Humor is another teaching device that improves learning. Research has shown that students best remembered material that was presented with a touch of humor. Their recall of humorously treated material was even superior to that of heavily emphasized material. Here again, we see the human factors in learning. You don't want to act like a clown, but an occasional light touch is pleasant and good pedagogy.

TELESCOPIC TEACHING

A fetish for "logical order" can impede learning. Teachers and students alike naturally assume that step one must be fully mastered before they can progress to step two. If that were strictly true, however, no child could speak without first developing a comprehensive vocabulary and a good knowledge of grammar.

The point here is that serial ordering is not necessarily best for learning—most often, a telescopic approach is superior. We learn faster and better by first seeing a central objective in outline form. Only then are the associated details seen in proper perspective; careful definitions, fine points, and subordinate steps all relate to the core point.

Am I suggesting that teaching should begin at the middle or end of a topic? Emphatically, yes! The idea seems strange because we imagine knowledge is only built brick by brick, in a logical, methodical, and linear manner. We pretend that learning is like an exercise in geometry, where we begin with definitions and axioms and develop lemmas and theorems in a tight chain of logical steps. This is a quaint notion that has little to do with the actual working of the human mind. Even in geometry, a theorem is first seen (some say "intuited") in nearly complete form; only then are linear steps constructed to prove it.

Of course, difficult concepts or procedures must await a complete development to be fully grasped. Nevertheless, almost any concept can be simplified enough to give the learner a framework on which to build. A full description of *entropy* requires some knowledge of probability theory and logarithms, but almost anyone can appreciate that "entropy is a measure of the disorder in a system."

The telescopic approach to teaching is nicely illustrated by good newspaper reports. Major points are summarized in the first paragraph, and elaborations are added as the article progresses. Similarly, a course in world history would introduce Alexander the Great with a brief description of his impact on history. Only then would details of Alexander's life and battles be presented. The traditional approach is just the opposite—as though the story might be spoiled by hearing the ending.

Perhaps problem-oriented subjects suffer most from the traditional linear approach. As lecturers plod through definitions and derivations, puzzled students plead to see an example. The students are right. When new concepts and principles are introduced in a transparent problem, students grasp the core of the theory. Refinements and elaborations then become meaningful and useful.

A telescopic approach to teaching should include, when possible, outlines and summaries of major units of instruction. These do not need to be detailed, but it is very desirable to let students know where they are going and where they have been.

Teaching requires planning and organization (even when it is spontaneous). Reveal your plans to your students. Clear objectives give purpose and direction to both the student and the instructor. Even more important, a student who knows the objectives has already learned a great deal.

DRESSING UP FACTS

Memorizing facts or terms is often dull and difficult. You can free students from this tedium by creating mnemonics with the techniques of visualization and association.

Students are familiar with acronyms and rhymes, but few are aware that visual associations are among the most powerful memory devices. Consequently, when you devise a visual mnemonic, you must instruct students to imagine the scene clearly and vividly.

You will find it more difficult to develop substitute images and associations for others than for yourself. When you create imagery for others, you cannot enjoy the complete freedom of your private thoughts or private meanings. Moreover, there are limits to how bizarre the associations may be, depending upon the sophistication of the students. These limitations can restrict your ability to create useful mnemonics.

Even with these restrictions, however, students can and do embrace quite imperfect substitute images. In an introductory art course, for example, early Greek columns are shown to have a three-part top or *capital*, consisting of *necking*, *echinus*, and *abacus*. The instructor told her students to visualize an animated column with small *caps* (for *capital*) attached to its *neck* (for *necking*), its *chin* (for *echnus*), and its *back* (for *abacus*). The students learned these, and a score of other architectural terms, immediately upon hearing them.

USING EXAMPLES AND PARALLEL PROBLEMS

It is good policy to illustrate your subject matter with plenty of examples. Research shows that simple examples work better than complex examples—probably because complications obscure the central point. Accordingly, use the simplest examples that illustrate your objectives.

Although examples are desirable in almost any subject area, they are virtually indispensible in problem-oriented instruction. One way students learn to solve problems is to see others solve them. A teacher can demonstrate a problem solution and ask the students to do another, highly similar problem. The key words here are "highly similar." Most students need to concentrate on emulating your solution; new elements in the parallel problem can cause confusion.

You can usually create parallel problems by changing any inessential element in the original. For instance, you might change numbers, symbols, or vary the information given and sought. The problem "Find how long it takes for a ball to fall twenty meters from rest" can be converted to the parallel problem "Find how far a ball falls from rest in two seconds." In both cases the principle and the relevant equation are the same.

Certainly, not all problems assigned to students should be parallel problems (except perhaps in elementary grades). Parallel problems do not test or extend students; rather, they provide practice in fundamentals and serve as models of good problem-solving technique.

TAKING SMALL STEPS

Chickens have been taught to dance! Not brilliant chickens—there are no brilliant chickens—but ordinary, barnyard hens have learned to turn and whirl on signal. The task was fragmented into tiny steps, and each step in the right direction was rewarded and reinforced. Ultimately, the sequence of steps completed the dance.

Many human learning objectives can also be broken into smaller, simpler objectives, and programmed instruction is predicated on such reductions. The technique is particularly effective for teaching computational and manipulative skills. For example, a martial arts instructor may teach an intricate kick by reducing it to component motions.

The small step technique is illustrated here with a problem in the arithmetic of complex numbers:

Problem: Find the product $(a + ib)(a - ib)$, where a and b are real numbers and $i^2 = -1$.

$i^2 = ?$	answer: -1
$(2i)(2i) = ?$	answer: -4
$(2i)(3 + 2i) = ?$	answer: $6i - 4$
$(2i)(3 - 2i) = ?$	answer: $6i + 4$
$(3 + 2i)(3 - 2i) = ?$	answer: 13
$(a + 2i)(a - 2i) = ?$	answer: $a^2 + 4$
$(a + bi)(a - bi) = ?$	answer: $a^2 + b^2$

Notice that each step is only a slight elaboration of the preceding step, and the sequence concludes with the original problem. Although the original problem may be difficult, the student should be able to perform each subordinate step.

This is a powerful approach, but it can be tedious and time-consuming. The small-step technique should therefore be limited to the more difficult or complex specific objectives.

QUESTIONING

Teaching is more effective when the instructor can establish a dialogue of questions and answers with students. Questioning has several features that make it a powerful tool.

Questioning requires students to take an active part throughout the session. Not surprisingly, research shows that learning improves with an increasing number of student responses.

Another virtue of continual dialogue is that students get immediate feedback—the desired answers are encouraged and others are discouraged.

Finally, the answers signal the instructor to adjust the approach to suit the students' needs. When a question appears too difficult, it can be simplified or broken into component parts. When a particular treatment is not working, an alternative can be chosen.

The technique of questioning is easily acquired. Simply ask students to perform any steps toward an objective that you expect are within their capability. You may feel no worthwhile purpose is served by asking questions that are easy to answer, but this is just the kind of exchange that creates student involvement. Of course, if the questioning is too trivial, time and energy are wasted. When this is the case, ask the students to handle only more significant steps. You will quickly sense the right level.

Your questioning should not resemble a third-degree or an oral exam. Use a casual and gentle approach.

Questioning works both ways. Give students' questions your fullest attention. If a question seems foolish or heading in the wrong direction, help the student formulate the question in a useful way. Respect and encourage students' questions.

SUMMARY

The Human Factors: Consideration and respect for students are important elements in effective teaching. Encourage students with praise and approval. Occasional humor in teaching helps students to remember.

Telescopic Teaching: Begin instruction with the most important idea or fact. Further refinements, details, and elaborations are then easily understood and retained. Reveal the organization of your teaching plans with outlines and summaries.

Dress Facts: Develop visual mnemonics for isolated terms and facts.

Examples: Fully illustrate topics with examples. Simple examples are more effective than complex ones.

Parallel Problems: Instruction in solving problems is assisted by demonstrating other, highly similar problems.

Small Steps: Difficult objectives can be broken into a sequence of smaller, simple objectives.

Questioning: Ask questions frequently and keep the student involved as an active participant. Most questions should be relatively easy for the student to answer.

20
NUMBERS

Learning telephone numbers,
prices, dates, and long numbers of all kinds

Numbers are notoriously difficult to memorize. A few numbers are easily remembered because they contain predictable sequences like *2468* or symmetrical patterns like *141414*. Most often, however, numbers are bloodless ciphers without pattern or visual appeal. The imaginative and visual half of the brain, the right hemisphere, therefore plays a reduced role in assimilating numbers.

Elaborate mnemonic devices have been developed to cope with the problem of numbers. One popular system was developed (as far as I can tell) by Dr. Bruno Furst and is widely used by modern mnemonists. This method assigns sounds to the digits; numbers then become words or word lists that are easily recalled. It is a powerful approach, but requires substantial practice to master.

The method presented here is more direct and can be thoroughly learned in one sitting. This technique of *animated digits* is as powerful as any for rapid learning. No doubt it is an old technique, but I have not seen it described explicitly.

THE TECHNIQUE
OF ANIMATED DIGITS

Once again we can discover a powerful memory technique by examining the approach of the incredible Russian mnemonist, Sheresheveskii. Unlike most of us, he found numbers to be the *easiest* items to remember, and he could memorize number lists without apparent limit.

Sheresheveskii regarded digits not as abstract symbols but as colorful characters. He saw the number 6 as a man with a huge swollen foot and 8 as a fat woman. Probably Sheresheveskii imagined long numbers as scenes being played by these digit-actors; the number 868 may be seen as two fat women crushing a man (with a swollen foot) between them. We can extend this basic idea to remember any number.

Press your imagination to see the following digits as characters and objects:

0   an egg
1   a soldier or palace guard standing at attention. (I see a red tunic and a huge hat.)
2   a floating swan with curved neck
6   a man with a swollen foot
8   a fat woman

Follow the imagery given here to remember the number 26102881600: A large swan has a man (with a swollen foot) riding on its back (26). This surprises a soldier sitting on an enormous egg, which breaks open and hatches a golden swan (102). The golden swan is promptly chased by two fat sisters and a soldier (881). In the chase, they step on a man's swollen foot, angering him and causing him to throw two eggs at them (600). Use vivid imagery, and recall the original number from your memory of the scenes.

Questions can arise regarding the order of the digits; do a soldier and an egg represent 10 or 01? A natural way to keep track is to place the character-digits in the same left-to-right positions as they occur in the number. If the number is 10, then the soldier is seen to the left of the egg. When you want the placements to be vertical—say a man riding a swan—have the character representing the first digit reach highest in the scene. Thus to represent 26 you imagine a man on a swan with the swan's head above the man's. (Of course, it is even easier to imagine 26 as a swan riding on a man's shoulders.)

Let the character-digits face any direction that suits you. A 2 looks like a swan facing left, but it can face right in any scene you imagine.

Exercise

Use the technique of this section to memorize the number 8012068216.

We can now complete the list of digits. Again, extend your imagination to see these:

0   an egg
1   a soldier or palace guard
2   a swan
3   a butterfly (the loops are wings)
4   a girl (her hand is on her hip so the bend in the 4 is her elbow)
5   a snake
6   a man (with a swollen foot)
7   a cane or walking stick
8   a fat woman
9   an elephant (the loop is its ear and the stem is its trunk)

Be sure to create vivid, unusual images. In your mind's eye a soldier can hatch from an egg, a butterfly can be as big as an eagle, and an elephant can lay eggs. Animated objects like an egg with legs or a talking cane are always useful elements. When possible, invent a story for each scene; the better the story, the stronger your recall. You can vary your character-digits by changing their color, composition, dress, and size. It also helps to see the numbers in groups (scenes) of two, three, or four digits.

Exercises

1. Use the technique of this section to memorize the number 6483591207.

2. Take a brief rest, and then give yourself three minutes to memorize the number 132315759408698072.

NUMBER ASSOCIATIONS

Useful numbers like stock prices or telephone numbers must be associated with the appropriate names. Numbers and names are easily linked by familiar techniques.

As an example, the telephone number of Mr. Frog is 890-3167. You can remember this by imagining that Mr. Frog kisses a fat woman (8) who is being pushed by an elephant (9), etc. This links Mr. Frog with his telephone number.

Exercises

1. Relate the following names and telephone numbers. Rehearse once for each and then cover the numbers and recall them from the names alone:

Mr. Frog	890-3167
Ms. Bear	420-5006
Dr. Owl	589-1366

2. Use the same approach as in Exercise 1 to remember the following historic dates:

Mohammed's flight from Mecca	622
Black plague reaches Europe	1347
Birth of Ludwig van Beethoven	1770

Cover the dates and recall them from the events.

By now you may have noticed that you remember many numbers even without a rehearsal. The technique promotes close attention and deep memory traces.

NUMBERS AS PEGS

Some mnemonists use numbers as memory pegs. One obvious advantage is that items are remembered in numerical order. To see how this works, suppose you want to remember a numbered list: (1) *table*, (2) *letter*, etc. you can visualize a soldier (1) growing out of a table, a swan (2) eating a letter, and so on. Multiple-digit items require composite scenes. For example, the item (10) *eyeglasses* can be seen as a soldier hatching from an egg (*10*) wearing eyeglasses (the soldier's head is above the egg, so *1* precedes *0*).

Exercise

To obtain a feeling for numerical pegs, associate the items below with the given numbers:

(1) table	(11) dog	(65) apple
(2) letter	(22) pencil	(78) microphone
(10) eyeglasses	(23) tree	(84) balloon

Now cover the list and recall the items associated with the following numbers: *11, 23, 84, 1, 2, 10, 22, 65, 78.*

The technique can be used to remember pages in a book or magazine. Page ten may have a picture and report on fashionable eyeglasses. You can associate *10* with this information, and when someone calls out "page ten," you can describe the contents of the page, including the layout and the photographs.

SUMMARY

Animated Digits: To remember numbers, visualize scenes with the digits as colorful characters or animated objects:

0 egg	5 snake
1 soldier	6 man
2 swan	7 cane
3 butterfly	8 fat woman
4 girl	9 elephant

Number Associations: Numbers can be associated with names by linking an image for the name to the number images.

Numbers as Pegs: By using the number images as pegs, items can be remembered in numerical order, and readings can be recalled by page number.

21
PERSPECTIVE

A few basic techniques
were adapted to many different applications

Throughout this book you applied techniques to numerous subjects. A close look shows that you used only a few basic techniques, and these were simply modified and combined for the various applications.

The cognitive sciences show that organization, visualization, and association are important—even essential—to learning. These principles are utilized in the three most fundamental techniques: telescopic thinking, substitute images, and memory chains. All other central techniques are variations and combinations of these.

Telescoping is our primary approach to organization. This hierarchical view is a hallmark of expert thinking; applying it purposefully to new material leads to dramatic learning. In the book the technique was applied directly to help you learn maps, processes, equations, and chemical structures. Telescoping is also the backbone of the core-equation approach that is so effective in problem solving.

Substitute images and memory chains together represent the basis for mnemonic systems based upon visualization and association. Some of the direct applications you saw included remembering people, learning English and foreign vocabulary, and learning technical terminology.

Special substitute images and chains are the basis for the technique for assimilating numbers.

The three basic techniques are combined to form a most useful learning instrument: the thought map. Here key words or images are organized in telescopic fashion, with layers of specifics linked in chains to a core point. Mapping is a central technique for reading, note-taking, and writing.

Finally, the memory peg technique is a variation of substitute imaging and chaining. It is particularly useful for learning while listening and viewing and for public speaking without notes.

Interest in learning techniques grows as the cognitive sciences reshape our view of the human mind. Years ago I did not imagine that such fast, effective learning was possible. Now I expect that learning techniques may gradually pervade textbooks, communications, and teaching with profound consequences for education and society.

INDEX